The Smile Behind the Pain

How Faith Turned My Wounds into a Witness

Anglore Chambers

Contents

Dedication

First and foremost, I dedicate this book to **God** for making all of this possible. My spiritual eyes are now wide open, and I have a full understanding of the journey I've been on. I see now that everything that happened was tied to my purpose. For a long time, I was confused and questioned God, but now I realize that I needed to trust the process.

To my husband, **Pastor Hugh Chambers**: You came into my life when I thought it was over, and you showed me what true love really is. You are my protector, my rock, and my confidant. You carry my burdens, you cook with such care, and most importantly, you are a great leader who respects and esteems women—something that means the world to me as someone who has struggled with domestic violence. You are dedicated, honest, and true, a humble man with a heart of gold. I've witnessed your selflessness as you pack your car with food and perishable items to deliver to families in need, feeding the homeless with compassion and love. You are my armor-bearer, and I am so grateful for you.

To my nine children—**Sydonie**, **Clair**, **Chris**, **Cleve**, **Erin**, **Najee**, **Renee**, **Hugh-Ann**, and **Hugh-Jay**: I love you all dearly. Everything I do is to extend my legacy to you. It hasn't been easy, but you've weathered the storm with me, and I am forever grateful.

A special acknowledgment to my firstborn, **Sydonie**: Your journey has been nothing short of remarkable. Serving in the military for 23 years with two Purple Hearts, you've shown incredible strength and bravery. Congratulations on your well-deserved retirement. It was nothing but God's grace that kept you safe in Iraq when your building was bombed and you temporarily lost your hearing. Yet, you persevered, and I must tell you how much I admire your resilience. The enemy didn't want you here, even from the time you were in my womb, but God kept you, and you are a walking miracle.

To my grandchildren and great-grandchildren, your mama loves you always.

To my granddaughter **Azara**: You represent my rebirth and my angel on earth. God placed you in my life when I was at my lowest, and you filled the void in my heart during a time of deep depression. Our bond is unlike any other, and I cherish it with all my being.

To **Dr. Odessa McNeil**: You have been a tower of strength and a vital part of my ministry. Thank you for jump-starting this journey with me. You were my Bible school professor and provided me with the materials that continue to guide my ministry today. Your support means more to me than words can express.

To my **congregation**: You believed in me, trusted my vision, and saw the God in me. You gave me a new definition of friendship and became the family I never had. I am so thankful for your unwavering support.

To all of our **donors** who help keep the ministry alive—**Amazo**n, **Second Harvest, Panera Bread, Toys for Tots, ShopRite, Walmart, Chipotle, Wawa, College Hill Presbyterian Church**, and **many others**—I appreciate each of you. Thank you for not just believing in the ministry but for serving tirelessly. Your contributions and generosity mean the world to me, and I love and appreciate you all.

Lastly, to my dear **readers**: Thank you for picking up this book and joining me on this deeply personal journey. I want you to know that every word written here is a testament to the grace of God, the power of resilience, and the strength that lies within all of us. My hope is that my story not only inspires you but also encourages you to keep pushing forward, no matter what challenges life may bring. You are not alone in your struggles, and if nothing else, I want this book to remind you that healing, purpose, and victory are possible. Trust your process, keep your faith strong, and never forget that your pain can become your purpose. Remember, there's power behind your smile.

I love you all. **Anglore**

Introduction

A smile. It's the most universal mask we wear. There is the smile that erupts from a place of pure, unadulterated joy, the one that reaches the eyes, that crinkles the skin, that feels like sunshine on your face. And then, there is the other smile. The one that is carefully constructed, a shield held up to the world, a fortress built brick by brick to hide the cracks of a broken heart. It's the smile you wear when you are hungry, when you are scared, when you feel utterly alone. It's the smile that says, "I'm fine," when everything inside you is screaming. This book is the story of that smile. It is the story of the pain I carried behind it for so many years and the incredible, unyielding power I eventually found there.

This journey begins on the sunny, vibrant, and beautiful island of Jamaica, a place of breathtaking beauty that also held for me the deepest of shadows. It winds its way through the cold, indifferent streets of America, a land that held the glittering promise of a better life but delivered some of my most harrowing trials. This is not a simple story of overcoming one or two obstacles. It is a raw and honest account of a life lived on the front lines of survival—a battle fought against poverty, homelessness, domestic abuse, serial heartbreak, and a debilitating chronic illness that threatened to steal what little strength I had left.

For years, I kept these stories locked away, buried deep beneath the surface of a life I was desperately trying to build. The shame, the pain, the fear—they were my secret companions. But God, in His infinite wisdom, does not allow our pain to be wasted. He takes the broken pieces of our lives, the very things we try to hide, and uses them to build a testimony. This book is my act of breaking the silence. It is my offering, my testament to the relentless grace of God and the incredible resilience of the human spirit. It is the story of how my greatest mess became my most profound ministry.

I will not sugarcoat the truth in these pages. You will walk with me through dark alleys of despair, you will feel the chill of lonely nights with nowhere to call home, and you will witness the sting of betrayal from those who should have protected me. It is not an easy journey to read, just as it was not an easy journey to live. But I promise you this: you will also witness the flicker of hope that refused to be extinguished. You will see the hand of God moving in the most unlikely of circumstances, and you will stand with me on the mountaintops of victory, celebrating the healing and restoration that can only come from a place of complete surrender.

This is more than my story; it is an invitation into yours. If you have ever felt broken, unseen, unworthy, or defined by your pain, then this book is for you. It is a reminder that even in our deepest suffering, there is a purpose waiting to be born, a strength waiting to be discovered. It is my prayer that by the time you turn the final page, you will not only understand my journey, but you will also recognize the incredible, unyielding power that lies behind your own smile.

Chapter 1

State of Innocence

It was 54 years ago on the beautiful island of Jamaica.

The setting was green trees with their branches hanging, loaded with fruits of different colors, tastes, and different names, farmers to and from their farms tending their cultivation and their stocks of animals, the birds of different species chirping as they flew from one tree to the next, making their nests and hatching their babies. The sun was hot and shining, as it glowed from the beautiful blue sky and as it reflected in the sea, and the sea dashed against the rocks. The sound was peaceful, and the rainbow color was romantic. The feeling of nature was romantic and appealing.

Men and women, boys and girls were in the market in the communities selling our favorite produce—Jamaican yellow yam, ackee, oranges, mangoes, vegetables, sugar cane, callaloo, and the list goes on. It was the smell of life. The music was inspirational and gave off a feeling of romance. The restaurants were booming with business, with their different refreshing island drinks, roast breadfruit, fried fish, and hot porridge. The carvers were carving their woodwork, making different pieces of art. The ladies were cutting and sewing. The scene was set, and it was beautiful.

But behind all this beauty and the looks of life, things were not so colorful for some residents. Things were very rough for some natives. In a very small community on the backside bushes of Jamaica called Bepthage, population of about 50, where everyone knows everyone, life was simple and comfortable. I was the fourth child of twelve siblings, but I was the first girl. I do not remember having a father around, only my mother, but things were good: a two-bedroom home, outside latrine, no electricity, no shower, and all hygiene was done in a wash basin behind the house. Everything was done manually, and life was good.

Our entertainment was sitting around at early evening hours, telling stories about ghosts (duppies) and characters such as Brotha Anancy aka the Jamaican version of "The Jeffersons" and Sanford and Son and other stories, and we would laugh ourselves to sleep. Every day we would look forward to this gathering. There was no radio, TV, or telephone. Every form of information was carried by word of mouth, no cars or bikes for transportation; everyone would walk. We would walk three miles to get water and had to carry it on top of our heads in a bucket, but life was still good. Our way for telling the time to get up in the mornings was when the rooster would crow; then we would know that it was time to get up. No one had a clock, watch, or any other means of telling the time. 12 noon—we would stand out in the sun, and if we were standing in our shadow, then we would know that it was noon time. The sounds of the crickets and other bugs would be our cue to tell us what time it was at night. Yet, life was still good.

Now as I look at all my accomplishments and all that has happened over the years, I can only wish that life could go back to those simple and natural ways of living as they were. According to Ecclesiastes (KJV)—Solomon, after living a life of success, a life of women and luxury, states that "Vanity of vanities—all is vanity and vexation of spirit." In life, we know that it is the ambition of every individual to be someone successful, to go to higher and deeper depths, to crawl, run, and eventually leap over boundaries, and to do whatever we can to help those who are less fortunate. I was no different. I had those ambitions. I was in my state of innocence. I cherished those thoughts and ambitions as a little girl in Bepthage. Even though at that time I had no idea what the outside world was like, I would see people come to visit from faraway places like Kingston and even the United States, and I would think and become very curious.

Finally, I began to notice that a gentleman, a very special gentleman, began to come to our home to visit my mother. But what was different about him from the rest, as there were others who would pass through as they were going to and from farming and would use our home as a rest stop for food and water and would then carry on. But this gentleman would come more often and stay longer. He was very nice to us, especially to my mother. But as I was very young, I could not process what was going on. But in the process of time, I realized that this was a nice man who had an interest in my mother; he was not there just to use our home as a rest stop, but he was there to take my mother away in marriage. My mother had already had 5 children, and it wasn't easy for her, and so this gentleman was like a prince who came to ask Cinderella's hand in marriage.

We were excited and ready for the move, which was about an hour away to another village. The day came, and we did not have much to take, so it was not hard to transport our belongings to our new village. Our only mode of transportation then was manually or by donkey, and so we successfully made the move on a weekday. Upon arrival to our new home, we met our new in-laws: Aunty J, who was in her 90s, and Uncle J, who was in his 70s. This new community was a more upscale community. I was so shocked to see that there was running water nearby. The rooms in the house were much bigger; there was more yard space around the home for playing, and so things seemed to be looking good for us with our newfound family. Not to mention that the grocery store was much closer to home; this meant less walking for the family.

But in life, not everything that glitters is gold; sometimes 'better' turns out to be worse. What seemed to be the beginning of a new and improved life turned out to be a master challenge for me. At this new home, there were three of my stepdad's nephews living there with him. Two occupied the room to the back of the house, and one shared the room with Grandma. Oh, this seemed to be lots of fun! Mom shared a room to the far left with my two new baby brothers and my sister, and I shared with Aunt J and Cousin Cee.

The sleeping arrangements: In this room was Aunt J's big bed, and I was very happy knowing that I was going to be sharing the same bed with Grandma. Not only was I going to share the same room with Grandma, but I felt rather special. Grandma Jane was very kind and welcoming and would pull us up into her bed to lie next to her, since she was bed-bound and unable to get out of bed. My mother, in addition to my stepfather, was her caretaker, and we did what we could to assist them in taking care of Grandma and Uncle J. At the age of eleven, we could not do much, but we did our best.

What my Grandma J did not know is that at nights, as I was sharing her bed with her, Cousin Cee wasn't just enjoying his newfound family; he was molesting me while I was sleeping. I would be awakened at nights and find my underwear down to my ankles and between my legs would be wet. At first, I had no idea what was happening to me. I thought that this was normal and that nothing was wrong, and so I said nothing to no one. Every night for the next three years, I would have this incident happen to me, not knowing how to make sense of it.

By the time I was about twelve to thirteen years old, my stepfather built a new home right above Aunt J's big house, and we all moved in. This was certainly a move in the right direction. Moving into a new home away from Cee was a blessing in disguise. Although we were still neighbors, Cee refused to face me or look me in my eyes. My mother was now officially married and had five more children, and so my responsibilities shifted to helping my mother with babysitting my siblings while my stepfather went out farming to provide food for the family.

There were times when I would have to go out farming with my stepfather, and days when I would have to stay home from school to assist with activities at home. Though I was at this point of frustration, I had the ambition to aspire to be something in life: to have a job that will enable me to help my mother and siblings to live a more comfortable life, a life that will enable her and my stepfather to stay home and raise their new family. But the constant reminder of what Cee did to me in Aunt J's big bed, as I got older and began to realize what really happened to me, began to confuse and frustrate me. I was silenced by my fear of the unknown and the painful experience. I kept on believing that it was my fault. Even if I opened up about the situation, I thought no one would believe me because we don't speak about these things in our family or community.

As I am sitting here writing, the pain of my past and the horrifying events are flowing down my eyelids by way of tears. The Bible (KJV) states in Psalm 38:9-10, "Lord, all my desire is before thee; and my groaning is not hidden from thee. My heart panteth, my strength faileth me: as for the light of mine eyes, it also is gone from me."

School for me was alright, but my focus was never truly on my education. Survival came first. Each day was filled with distractions—fetching water early in the morning, farming with my stepfather, and taking care of household duties. I had to wake up by 5 a.m. to fetch water, filling up the drum so we had enough for the day, before embarking on the long walk to school. On some days, I couldn't attend school at all because I had to help on the farm. Balancing these responsibilities made it hard to concentrate on my studies, and over time, my academic performance suffered. Despite my efforts, I didn't do well in school. By the time I reached the ninth grade, which was the highest grade in primary school, I knew that my chances of continuing were slim.

I had tried to earn a scholarship to high school through sports, but unfortunately, I didn't make it. At 15, I had one last chance to pass the Grade Nine Achievement Test, but when I didn't succeed, my formal education was over. If you didn't pass that test, there was no moving forward. For me, that was the end of my schooling. Finances played a big part in this. My mother was raising a new family, and while she wanted to see me excel, there simply wasn't enough money to invest in my education. Without a father in my life, I had no other support to turn to.

At 16 years old, I felt like my future was over. My dreams of a better life seemed out of reach. I continued to help my stepfather on the farm, and while I enjoyed the simple pleasures of cooking over a wood fire and eating a large meal at the end of the day, there was little to look forward to. The weight of my unfinished education and the limited opportunities ahead of me felt like an insurmountable burden. Life, at that point, felt stagnant, and the dreams I once had begun to fade away.

SELF REFLECTION QUESTIONS:

Who made you feel most seen as a child, and what did they do that told you "you matter"?

When did your innocence first feel challenged, and what changed in your body, your home, or your world?

When you think of your earliest "safe place," what do you see, hear, and smell?

If your inner child could make a request of you today, what would it be—and how will you meet it this week?

Finish these sentences:

"When I was little, I felt safest when _____."

"The child in me still believes _____."

"To protect my peace now, I will _____."

Chapter 2

The Red Shoe Experience

At this point in time, I was very angry.

On a bright weekday morning, I walked out to the only store in the community. As I stood there, I recognized a gentleman at the post office window. He was the overseer for the Public Works Department Headquarters at the main office in town. I boldly walked over and introduced myself to him in broken English. "Sir, good day. I just left school, and I am not working. Could you please assist me in getting a job with the Public Works Department?" He replied, "As a matter of fact, we are looking for someone to work in the Claremont office. If you are willing to commute, the job could be yours."

My mouth dropped wide open. I pinched myself. This can't be real, I thought. But yes, it was broad daylight, and I was wide awake, speaking to this gentleman. Go for it! I told myself. He gave me the details right then and there, telling me to go downtown to another office in another community to register with them. I would start working the following week. Oh, dear God, what a miracle! I ran home to my mother and told her all that had happened. She smiled with approval and gave me her blessings.

As the days went by, I became more excited. It had never crossed my mind that this might not be all that it appeared to be. I stayed focused on the offer and how much my life was going to change for the better. I had no experience outside of home, no knowledge, no exposure that would equip me for the job, but I was ambitious. It never crossed my mind to even question the important experiences that I would need for the job offer.

The week went by, and the weekend prior to my start date on Monday, I left home to stay with my maternal grandmother, who was living two miles away from where the new job was located. So, I went to stay with her while working and would go home on the weekends to my mother. This seemed to be a well-thought-out plan, one that would solve all of the problems that I was encountering: the sexual abuse at such an early age, not being able to tell my parents, and having to live right next door to the man who molested me for so long. Oh, how all of this is going to go away now. This is the answer to my wishes. At the time, I had no idea who God was, so I would wish and believe that all good things were because of luck.

In life, and looking over my own life, I had never seen or heard of anyone planning or preparing for bad times. We were always looking forward to better and good times. But the truth is that in the midst of good times, there were always bad times ahead—bad times that can leave an impact that can destroy a whole community. It never entered my mind that this was the beginning of a journey that was paved with much trouble on every side.

Monday morning, bright and early, I got dressed and headed to my new position with the Department of Public Works. There, for the first time on any job, I met coworkers and supervisors and was formally welcomed. I felt very comfortable. I sat at my desk and, surprisingly, I was given my assignment. Now that I am looking back at the task given to me, I realize I received no orientation. I had to find my way around. At that moment, I realized I wasn't going to make it. I had no idea what they were doing or talking about. The language was totally different. I felt as though I was in a strange country. I was most definitely uninformed and unequipped. I felt like a soldier at war with no weapon to defend myself.

At that moment, I suddenly realized that this was not it. I was done, it was over, and I was back to square one. The next day, I was asked to leave. Being inexperienced was my demise, so I was soon replaced. I did, however, continue staying with my grandmother, which, now that I looked back, was a part of my destiny.

Things didn't work out very well there. There had been some previous disagreements with the family. My grandmother didn't really think much of my father, whoever he was, and so she carried a small grudge for him, which spilled over on me. That meant I was not one of her favorite grandchildren. While living with Grandma, I had time to get involved in other things, and so I began going to one of the local churches. I accepted Christ, got baptized, and started going to church. But there was one problem: I didn't have any clothing or shoes to go to church, but I was managing somehow.

The moment arrived when they were having a special event, our church's anniversary. This occasion was to be a 'dress-up' event. I was excited to attend but didn't have the funds I needed to purchase my clothes for this special day. This was the very first time that I would be getting dressed up for any occasion. So, I was anxious and was looking forward to being a part of this special occasion.

I set out on a wild goose chase, asking everyone for their monetary support to purchase the attire that I needed to wear to this anniversary. I was blessed with a dress but had no shoes to wear. On the norm, it would not be a problem to go barefoot, but this occasion was too special to attend without shoes. My last chance was my step-grandfather, who told me yes, that I should go to Grandma and tell her that when she was finished shopping on Saturday, to give me whatever was left of the money to get my shoes.

Oh, hallelujah! I was finally getting everything ready, and I knew that I was going to be special at this event. I ran inside and told Grandma what Grandpa said. My heart fell into my stomach at Grandma's reply when she answered, "No!" Time was running out. What do I do now? Suddenly, I remembered that there was a middle-class family living in the community that seemed as though they were rich. They had a son by the name of Daniel, about my age, and I had this brilliant idea that I would ask him for a loan to purchase my shoes. I felt so confident in my mind that this was now going to work. I felt as if I already had the shoes, and so I went to Daniel and posed the question to him. He replied, "Yes, I will buy the shoes, but you will have to give me some (sex) first."

And yes, I agreed. The Word of God in Hosea 4:6 (KJV) says, "My people are destroyed for lack of knowledge: because thou hast rejected knowledge, I will also reject thee, that thou shalt be no priest to me: seeing thou hast forgotten the law of thy God, I will also forget thy children." I had no idea that this was wrong. My own conscience convicted me, letting me know that we were not married, or responsible enough as yet to be engaging in such activities, for the penalties and consequences that followed would be damaging, and so I gave it no second thought.

As an immature youngster, I was only about 18 years old and decided to take on this great decision, not knowing anything about this depth of intimacy or protection against the dangers of teen pregnancy, diseases, and fornication: sinning against the temple of God. We planned to meet at nighttime when my grandmother was asleep in my room. This plan was a success. No one discovered or heard this young man entering my room. That night he spent about twenty minutes with me because we were both very much afraid, and I gained my present, which was the money for my pair of red shoes. No one in my family asked me where I got my pair of red shoes, and I did not volunteer this information to anyone. After all, they did not care, so I thought.

The event was a great success. As I can remember clearly, the blessing of the Lord was poured out upon us in a great way. The night ended in a beautiful atmosphere of peace and love. I left for home feeling as if something great was accomplished and a spirit of contentment upon me. Here at home, things continued to be quiet. I would try to find things outside the home to do or places to go, which wasn't much, until I met a beautiful and kind lady by the name of Esther. Esther was very happy and smart.

One day, I sat down with her and began to tell her about my life. She was very sympathetic and to my amazement, she asked if I would like to come live with them. She stated that she has a craft shop where she makes straw hats and baskets and could use the help. I was utterly blown away by her offer. I did not think I was worth her while and wondered why she wanted to help me; furthermore, she doesn't know me. But I gladly accepted the offer and immediately moved into her lovely home with her and her daughter.

Esther was a hard worker and very productive. She also had a farm in addition to her craft shop, and we would get up early in the mornings to tend to the chickens, pigs, and goats. We would have breakfast and then open the craft shop. I felt as though I was born into this family and was beginning to get very comfortable.

Two months after being there and already settled, my world came crashing down on top of my head in an instant. No, no, no—I was feeling nauseous, and as I stepped outside the doorway, I began to vomit. But this vomiting was different. Despite the fact that I was inexperienced, something felt wrong. The color of the vomit was green, and it was a bitter taste. It was not from any food that I may have eaten, and so it was just all liquid. But I thought, Maybe I did eat something that upset my stomach? No, I answered. Could it be that I was pregnant? I knew it was only twenty minutes and it was two months ago. I did not say anything else to anyone. I decided to observe what was happening to me to see if it would happen again.

The day went by, but I was not feeling well. I was tired and wanted to sleep. I went to bed early that night, very troubled in my mind. Esther noticed that I was quiet and asked if I was alright. "Yes," I replied. The next morning, I was awakened by this same feeling of nausea, and I began to vomit again. Esther came out and asked me again if everything was ok. I said no, I am feeling sick, and two mornings in a row, I kept vomiting this green liquid that was very bitter. She looked at me and asked if I'd had any sexual relationship with anyone. I said yes, ma'am. She said that's a sign that you are pregnant.

I felt as if I was on a long journey, walking, looking for my destination, and could not find my way out. What will I do now? What would I tell my mother? I know without a doubt that I could not stay here in this lady's home while pregnant. She was kind enough to give me a place to stay, free of charge, and look at what I did. The feelings of shame, guilt, loneliness, and rejection began to flood my mind. This was not what I wanted for me. I wanted to make my mother proud, but I kept hitting rock bottom, and now this. Who will I tell them the father was? I could not tell them what I did for those red shoes...and with who...and where.

There is an old saying that anything that happens in the dark will eventually come out in the light. Esther said very little. I was pretty sure she was just as disappointed as I was. And I realized that since she was not inviting me to stay and she was not coming up with any solutions, I was on my own, because silence certainly always means consent. I decided that the only option that I have at this time was to go back home to my mother's house. But what do I tell them? How do I explain to them why I'm home? I felt worthless and inadequate. I began to look back; I was molested, I did not accomplish anything in school, I could not even keep that job, and now look at what happened to me for a pair of shoes. Everything that I aspired to be now descended into the drain in twenty minutes. Now I was going to be a mother. I needed to grow up real fast, but where and how? The questions kept coming in but no answers to them, for the fear of the unknown was brewing in my mind.

SELF REFLECTION QUESTIONS:

When did you first put on something that made you feel powerful or "seen"? What were you chasing—and what were you hiding?

What do "red shoes" symbolize for you right now—freedom, rebellion, attention, survival, or something else?

What was the cost of wearing your "red shoes," and what did you gain?

Recall a moment when the spotlight felt good until it burned.

If you could hand those "red shoes" to your younger self, what blessing or warning would you whisper before she steps out?

Chapter 3

Kicked Out and Finding Rescue

It was on a Saturday morning, bright and early.

I sat with Esther and told her that I had appreciated all that she had done, but that at this point I must leave. I did not expect her to take care of all my problems for me, and so, once again, I packed my bags and I left to go back home to mother. I had no idea how this was going to work, but I must leave. How the reception would be, I truly didn't know, but I must journey. I began to make up stories in my head of what to tell my mother when I got home.

The journey was not too long. It was only a 45-minute ride, and so I took off for home. I got home and mother, as usual, was in the kitchen. I walked up the yard space and greeted her; "Hi mother!" "How-di-do," she said. It seemed as if she had already heard something but said nothing. Silence followed, then I walked into the two-bedroom half-finished house, still waiting to hear mother ask me why I'm home, or anything to break the ice, but of course, she said nothing.

I went inside and lay down, of course very tired from the pregnancy and the fear of the unknown. My siblings were very happy and so we talked and gave jokes as usual. Night came and we all went to sleep. Fear of the unknown haunts me. At daybreak, I began to feel nauseous, and I went outside to vomit as usual. Mother heard what I could not hide, as she came out to let me know that she knew I was pregnant, and unfortunately there was not enough space for me to stay there. So she suggested I stayed with a friend of hers that lived over the hill, about a half a mile away from home. I was not happy about that idea, but I had no other choice, and considering the circumstance, I understood. Mom further offered to assist with providing meals and whatever else she could provide.

As the days and weeks passed, I would go over to this little house at nights where I would sleep, and then came home to my mother's house early in the mornings to have coffee. One morning I came home and stood by the kitchen waiting for my cup of coffee. As I received the cup of coffee in my hand and was about to take a sip, a hand came out of nowhere and grabbed the cup of coffee out of my hands. Then a voice said, "I told you not to come home anymore," as I looked up and realized it was my stepfather. I pushed back and resisted him. Then I ran through the house and out into the yard towards the fenced yard next door, jumped the barbed wire and fell to the ground, and rolled down the hill in an attempt to kill myself.

My mother, who was now in a frenzy, came running towards the fence. She picked me up and rushed me to the doctor. To my amazement, I was fine, not even a scratch. I was three months pregnant at the time, but my unborn baby was also fine. Today, I love my stepfather very much and realized out of frustration that was just his way of dealing with all that was happening to the family.

During that time, I had no prenatal care, as in those days prenatal care was not as it is today. The only care I had from a doctor was when I had the fall. There was no money to prepare for the birth of the unborn baby. After the fall, I had a surprise visitor; a lady from the community, who was a school teacher, had heard about my story; as we live in a very small community, came to see my mother, and made an offer to us. She needed someone to stay at her home with her newborn baby, and if I was able to do this, she would pay me a salary and give me a place to stay until I have my baby.

This seemed like a bright idea. This would enable me to pay for some doctor's visit and be able to buy the necessary items needed for my baby. I packed my bag with my few pieces of clothes and took off to my new home and second place of employment. Oh my, this place was picture perfect. Her home looked like a home you see on TV; a palace that no one has ever walked in or used. My room was in the same room with the baby, very comfortable. Thank God I can rest and make the necessary preparation that my unborn baby deserved and no one would bother us. After all, I would be home alone during the day. I could catch up on some of the things that I needed to take care of.

I was oriented to the home and what my duties would be and when I would be paid. The table was set and ready to go. My first day began and it ended very well. Baby James was very cuddly and friendly. As the days and weeks turned into months, I noticed that I wasn't getting paid, and my workload was increasing every day. But the interesting part of the whole new deal was that my employer's brother began to come over for visits during the day when no one was at home, and his visits were becoming more frequent, and he was beginning to be very friendly.

Time was going and I still hadn't received any payments for my services. I was not only a babysitter but now I was also the housekeeper, the cook and the brother's sex toy. During the days while I was home, Dexter would come over to visit and would have sex with me and then leave before his sister got home.

The time had arrived; June 1975, when I received a note from my mother stating that she spoke to Nurse Smyth who was the Nurse midwife for the community center, who stated that I was to come down to her home until the birth of my baby. But since I still had not received any payments from my employer, there was no preparation for the delivery of my unborn baby. The following day I packed my few pieces of clothing, once again, and headed out to Nurse Smyth's home.

This was not unusual for Nurse Smyth to take in young girls into her home prior to their giving birth so that she could monitor them, especially when they had no prenatal care. At Nurse Smyth's, I was warmly welcomed. She made sure I ate and rest. She would remind me that I needed to get myself prepared for giving birth, which would not be easy.

I stayed at Nurse Smyth's home for about six days, then suddenly I went to the bathroom and wiped myself, there was blood. Then I began feeling cramps in my lower abdominal region. That was when I realized that the baby was about to come. I went out and called Nurse Smyth and immediately she told me to get in bed, at which point she examined me and told me yes, it was time, and it was a big one.

As the evening got closer, I began to feel more discomfort in my abdomen. I could hear Nurse Smyth talking to herself as she checked the status. The pain began to get increasingly worse as I grew more uncomfortable. Then I noticed a look of concern on Nurse Smyth's face. She says, "I am having some trouble with...," then she stopped. Then she said, "This is a big one, I have to go over to the clinic for a minute. I will be back in a second."

She left and returned in a minute just like she had said, with an instrument of some sort. She said she did not know why my abdomen was separated; it was in two halves. "This part, the baby is down here, and there is a little middle right here, and something is up here," as she continued to speak to herself.

It was almost nine hours later, and the pain was becoming more severe. Then I heard Nurse Smyth talking to herself again, and laughing out loud saying, "Now I see what is happening. Her urine needs to come out, this is all water." I could feel when she inserted the instrument, and something warm gushed down my leg. Then she began to laugh again and said, "Any minute now girl, hang on," with a deep Jamaican accent. "I knew this water that was backing up in your belly, but it is out now. It is going to be over soon," she reassured me.

The pain became unbearable, and then she began telling me to push. I felt as if I was going to die, as my whole body began to rip apart and my back felt like it was opening in two. "I can see the head now," she said. "Stay strong, and with all that you have left, just push." Suddenly I felt as though I was split in half, as she told me the head was out. I had no more strength. She said to me, "Relax for a minute. Let me make sure…" then she paused as usual.

Then the pain came again and once more she instructed me to push. She said "It is a girl, and she is beautiful! Oh my, this is a big one, and everything is fine." Nurse Smyth looked at me as I began to cry. Laying there in the bed with a brand-new baby girl, a bundle of joy, I am now beginning to remember, that once this is all over, I had nowhere to live.

Nurse Smyth left the room and came back and said, "She weighed nine pounds and four ounces. Dear God, girl you didn't look that big, where did you carry her?" As I looked at her in amazement, I saw that she was exceedingly beautiful. Then the moment came when Nurse Smyth asked, "So who is picking you up? When are you leaving?" I paused for a second before answering, and then I asked her, "When do I have to leave?" She said "Normally, if everything is fine with you and the baby, we keep you for three days, as long as all is we."

I tried my very best to avoid the question, because she had no idea that myself and this baby girl had no place to lay our heads once we left her home. Matthew 8:20 (KJV) "And Jesus saith unto him, the foxes have holes, and the birds of the air have nests; but the Son of man hath not where to lay his head." And so, at this moment, I needed to think really fast what my next move was going to be, and so a brilliant idea came to me that I should write a note and send it to Esther; that same lady that gave me a home to stay before I discovered that I was pregnant. After all, that is my only hope. The only thing that she can say is either yes or no.

The following morning as I lay there, I began to count down the days, as they began to go by fast. It is amazing when you are facing trials, how time seems to move fast towards the unknown. I asked Nurse Smyth for a pen and paper, and I wrote a note to Esther. My younger sister who attended school in the same community, stopped in to visit on her way home, and so I gave her the note to give to Esther. Lord this was my only hope, and I did not know what she was going to say, after all, I hadn't seen her since I left her home. Dear God, I wondered if she was still upset with me.

As I waited for the answer, I now began to realize that I did not have any clothes for this newborn baby or any kind of blankets that a brand-new baby needed. After all, I never got paid, so I wasn't able to make any preparations. The hours were getting closer for my sister to bring back words. School was out and she would be here any minute now. As I counted down the time, my heart began to pound and my palms began to sweat.

Finally, I heard when Nurse Smyth opened the door and said, "Good evening beautiful, are you here for your sister?" She said "No, I came to give her something." As I opened the note, cold sweat began to pour down my face and neck. Oh dear, thank You, thank You, she said yes. Esther said that I could come back and live at her home, both me and the baby. The next morning, Esther picked us up and we went home. We received a warm welcome by the whole family. They fell in love with the baby instantly and the eldest daughter decided what she was going to name her. She named her and gave her a middle name.

But wait, "Who is her father?" They asked. I paused and gave a name of a gentleman in the community where my mother lived. This gentleman had the same last name as my daughter's biological father and was a close friend to me while I was going through. So, one of my plans was to avoid telling what happened the night I received my shoes. I planned to tell them that this gentleman, who was much older, was my baby's father, which he did agree to go along with it. And it did work for the moment or at least for some time.

I did not realize that the very decision I was making at the time was the very same thing that happened to me. I am not really sure what my mother's reason was for giving me another man's name other than my own father's, but I was not given my rightful surname. I was never told who my real father was. For many years I was led to believe that my father was someone else, and I continued to believe that until I was told by a family member, that this man who I called father was not my real dad. When I finally pursued and reached out to my real dad, I was rejected and scolded.

My daughter was given this other man's name and it was received by everyone. The only ones that knew the truth was myself and this gentleman, and he went right along with it out of pity for me. Despite the fact that my mother went after him for child support, he said nothing. John went right along with the lie with me and showed patience, consideration, and long suffering, to avoid further humiliation, embarrassment, and pain on my behalf.

This gentleman; John, was ten years my senior. He also helped himself sexually with me in the first trimester of my pregnancy. That was my reward to him for keeping my secret. In my journey, I learnt that nothing in life was free. There was a price for everything. Sometimes the price was very costly. Thank God for His redeeming blood that was shed as this ultimate payment.

At Ms. Esther's house, we were enjoying the open welcome and the homely atmosphere. But one thing that I did not pay careful attention to was Esther's stepson who was now living there at the house with Esther and their children. His name was David and appeared to be very low keyed. He did not say much but was always smiling. He noticed a lot moving about the home quietly and was shy about him. It was not easy to catch up with him; he had a very kind of slippery behavior. I paid very little attention to these movements.

I adjusted myself to the family quickly and began to call Esther's mother, and her husband daddy, and for all I knew, we were a family and I am happy. In life, never take anything for granted. Our God-given gifts are always to use our common sense, to look twice, and to pay attention to everything. Some things are just too good to be true. I never gave David a second thought. I went along with my daily activities, taking care of baby Syd.

Now she was blessed with blankets, clothes, baby formulas, and wasn't in need of anything. Esther made sure I was a good mother to baby Syd, and so she made sure I took care of myself, in regards to post-partum care. She was all that a daughter and granddaughter could ask for. But little did I know that the devil was not finished with me as yet. My troubles had just begun, for right in this safe haven of my new home; Satan was waiting to use my inexperience to overthrow me.

In addition to that, what the devil meant for evil, God knows just how to turn it around for good, for purpose was at work. My journey was not finished at Esther's home. It had just begun. I was too comfortable and so David was placed in that home and awaited my grand entrance the second time around to derail me and send me on my journey to finish my assignment and to push me into my destiny.

King James Version; Jeremiah chapter 1- God told Jeremiah, that before you were conceived in your mother's womb, I called you, I sanctified you, and predestined you for such a time as this. Too many times, when we are called by God, we have the audacity to believe that our assignment is going to be one of luxury and comfort. Many of us believe that God wants to use people who have all their I's dotted and their T's crossed.

I will have the churches to know that God still has a classified ad looking for whosoever will and is still willing to stand the test of time to fulfill the scriptures in these last days. In the days of old, Paul was willing, John was willing, Peter was willing and many, many more. They faced perilous journeys and risked their lives for the gospel and eventually suffered martyrdom by fire and vicious animals, and today are no different.

Satan the counterfeit, imposter also have an ad in the advertisement column looking for whosoever will to do his dirty trickery and deceptive job to derail God's assignment for His people, and very sad to say, there are a lot of volunteers that are willing to apply to Satan's offer, and do a great job on his behalf, and many of the applicants, sad to say, are our very loved ones whom we love so dearly.

It was a beautiful Sunday morning and at Esther's home, everyone would go out to church, but because baby Syd was still very young, I was allowed to stay home with her. But unbeknown to me, David stayed home too. I thought nothing of it until he approached me in a sexual manner. This kind of invitation opened the door for trouble that I was not aware of at the time.

Almost all the time when you are too comfortable, you don't catch on too fast. Things have a way of passing by without notice. But David began to get closer and closer, and I began to love it. The attention was very appealing and made me feel even more special. Not only was I now a part of this family, but now being looked at as a sex object, and so in the process of time, a sexual affair started with me and David.

Still not knowing anything about birth control, I laid myself careless and started a secret affair with David. I was truly enjoying this affair, but this did not continue too long, because within months I began to vomit that same bitter, green liquid substance that I vomited when I first discovered that I was pregnant with baby Syd. Oh, dear Jesus, I would've said, had I really known who Jesus is then. Could it be that I was really pregnant again.

I was standing in the same place that I stood 13 months ago, vomiting again. At this point baby Syd was only now about 5-6 months old. This was only a dream, and I was having a nightmare. I began to think, but no, I was standing in the same spot, and I was vomiting. What could I tell her this time? Esther was going to kill me. I must leave right now, but oh my God, where would I go this time? This was my fault.

I was so confused. I didn't know what to do, so I hurried inside and told David what was happening. His reply was not much. He just looked at me and hung his head down and walked away. I was now left with the decision to make. Where do I go from here? All that we did know for sure was that we were in big trouble. Esther was going to put us through the ringer and squeeze us dead.

I was thinking, not only that the shame and gossiping that would come with this new pregnancy, haven't I learned anything the first time around, how could this be? I was not even completely over my first drama with what had happen, then how was I going to deal with this new one? But time was now going and a decision had to be made concerning this situation.

As I began to exhibit the same nauseous feelings that I had before, it was very obvious to Esther and the family what was happening, but everyone was very quiet. David and I decided the second time around that we must leave and so we both talked with Esther and told her that we were leaving. With nowhere in mind, we packed our bags and headed off West, to the main town; Claremont, then South towards Spanish Town where David's mother lived.

On our way, while hitchhiking, we stopped at Aunt F who lived halfway between our journey. Upon arrival we saw her standing by the wayside, and she smiled and welcomed us. We were happy for the welcome. We made it seem as if we just came to visit her for a couple of days. We hid everything from her and so we were welcomed as her guests.

She took us up to her two bedrooms home and gave us her bed to lie in so that we could rest after the journey. She had no idea I was pregnant. But I was very grateful, and so I received the royalty treatment as long as it lasted, since I knew it was going to be temporary. She took out her best bed spread and made her bed up for us and we went to sleep. If only she knew our story.

She went to the little kitchen outside, made up her wood fire, and cooked up a meal, and we did eat to our heart's content. But as we discussed among ourselves, what we would do when she found out that we were pregnant and homeless. She would tell us to leave because it was obvious that she could not help us. She was obviously looking for help herself.

Finally, a couple of days turned into weeks, and we were forced to tell her the truth about our situation. "Sorry, I would love to help you but as you can see that we have no room and I am not working so you will have to find a place to stay," she replied. We were not surprised as this was the kind of response we were expecting to get, and so the next morning we packed our bags.

We had no money, and we were not really sure if our destination to be; which was David's biological mother whom I have never met, would receive us. On top of that, David hadn't seen or spoken to her in a long time. After all, he left her in the first place, because times were hard, and he left to find work to help her. But as we hitch hiked towards her home, the journey was long and hard.

Sixty miles ahead of us, walking and hitch hiking with baby Syd in hand with no food. Finally, we were picked up by a kind stranger who dropped us close to our destination. We were now about thirty miles from home as I became very tired and began to cry. David was compassionate, and so we sat and rested on the sidewalk, before resuming our journey.

Finally, towards dark, we reached our destination; home, or so we thought. As usual, the welcome was one of love and warmth. But things did not look like what I expected. You could immediately see the look of poverty everywhere. It was obvious that drought was a problem because the grass around the house and outside the yard was dry and the dirt in the yard was dry and hard.

The house was just one big open space with no individual rooms; the door separating the rooms was just an old sheet. I also noticed an old pit toilet located to the left of the house, and that was very important to me, since I needed the use of a bathroom more often due to my pregnancy. I looked around but did not see a place for a shower and so I just stood there at a loss for words.

I began to journey back in mind to all the events of my life and the things that had happened, and how I could've prevented all of this that was happening now. But all I could do was begin to cry within. David and his mother began to talk about his experiences back in St. Ann where he lived for the past couple of months. It was then that I became even more fearful and nervous. The languages were not very inviting.

Boy was I in for a treat, with a toddler to raise and an unborn child in my womb. What's next, where do I go from here? Where was I going to sleep? There was no place for privacy and no running water. This was the worst of all the other experiences, and most of all, what were we going to eat? It was very obvious that food was not something that was of ease of access around here.

This was a place where every tub had to sit on its own bottom, in terms of everything. So, I was on my own, I said to myself. But I was pregnant! Then I thought to myself, so what? Who cares? I was not even offered a glass of water, glass? From where? Nor something to eat, eat? From where? I said to myself again.

Then I sat on the wooden step of the house, which seemed as if it hadn't been cleaned for years, and I began to stare up into the sky thinking, maybe I would see someone just appear and come and take me away from all that was happening, but I realized very soon that that was just wishful thinking. Night came quickly and suddenly like a brick to the face, and the lighting in the house was very poor.

My sleeping spot was in the open room on a little bed while David was on the opposite side with his brother and others that I did not know. There was nothing to eat. The only way to get something to eat was to go and beg. As the time passed, things got increasingly worse. Then David began to get violent, and he began to beat up on me. He would fight me.

At one point he punched me in my mouth and knocked out my teeth. This kind of behavior became an everyday thing. I would go outside and hide in the pit toilet and cry. There was no one to talk to. My pregnancy was not even a concern since it really did not matter. No one knew that I was pregnant since I used to use pieces of clothing to tie my belly down.

I know that I did not do everything right, but dear Lord, why are these things happening to me? In the process of time, as the beating continued, there was neither food nor a real place to live. I suddenly decided I really don't care what was going to happen, but I decided that I must find a way to make it back home to my mother. Even if I had to sleep outside, which I knew that she would not allow me to do.

I told David what my decisions were, and he gave me the ok to go home. The next morning, I packed my bags of nothing and headed into town to the bus terminal. I spoke to the bus driver and told him I did not have any money to pay my fare to go home, and he told me it was alright, he would give me a free ride home.

The bus ride was long and tiresome with baby Syd in my hand and the unborn baby in my stomach. It was not an easy task, and not to mention the fact that I hadn't eaten in so many days. My mind was now in overdrive wondering what I was going to say to my mother when I got home. My abdomen was wrapped so that no one could see that I was pregnant. So that was taken care of, but just getting a place to lay my head was the most important thing at this time...

The bus arrived in St. Ann at about 5:00 P.M. I got out and stood on the sidewalk waiting for transportation to get home to my final destination three miles away into the country. Embarrassment and shame washed my face as I hid behind the light post and empty cars on the street corners, praying to God that no one I knew would see me.

As the 5:30 bus arrived in my direction, I hopped on it fast, without bus fare and asked if I could ride the bus for free since I had no money and was not able to walk home with baby Syd. Again, I was allowed to ride for free. After an hour ride, I was finally home. I walked up the driveway and up into the yard. "Good evening mama." "Lawd, evening, weh yuh come from now?" She asked. "Spanish Town mam." "So, a when yuh a go back??" (In Jamaican broken English) I responded, "I am not going back, because I have no place to stay."

She said you know that you cannot stay here, but you could go stay with your uncle up in Bensonton. Oh, what a brilliant idea. My uncle lived about three miles away from my mother's home and as far as I can remember, uncle was always one who was very pleasant and jovial, very simple and always ready at the drop of a dime to assist anyone in need. Oh what? Why didn't I think of him before? I knew that he would help me.

Then I suddenly remembered the concealed pregnancy that was hidden and bandaged down with a piece of towel. At times the band was so tight that I could hardly breathe, but I managed. At times, due to the present events, I forgot that I was carrying a baby in my womb, but of course it was obvious that that was the very least of my current problem. Once I lay my head somewhere, anywhere, then I would be able to give this pregnancy some thought.

SELF REFLECTION QUESTIONS:

When have you felt unwelcome or displaced, and how did you respond in that moment?

What does "home" look and feel like to you right now—physically, emotionally, and spiritually?

Who are three people or places that feel safe when everything else feels uncertain?

What belief about your worth tends to surface when doors close—and what truth will you choose instead?

If rescue arrived today, what form would it take—and what first step can you take to meet it halfway?

Chapter 4

The Cover-Up

I woke up worried yet optimistic as I set sail to continue my journey off to my uncle, on foot, 35 miles away, with baby Syd on my hip. I hitchhiked my way to my uncle's house. Finally, I arrived, and I told him what I wanted him to hear (or what he wanted to hear) enough for him to permit me to stay, at least for a while. I made no mention of my concealed pregnancy to him.

Uncle took me inside his house, which had only one bedroom, a living room, an outside kitchen, and a pit toilet to the side. He said, "There's a little bed here in my room. You can use it with the baby as long as you want." I thanked him and made myself at home. Food was not a problem as my uncle was a farmer, so we always had provisions but not meat, but I was grateful. We could get coconut along with cabbage and callaloo and improvise.

So, life was good. There were fresh oranges, grapefruit, and apples, so I ate to my heart's content, along with baby Syd. We did not have to worry about shoes and clothes; it really was not a necessity, so we were content with what little we had. As baby X grew in my stomach, I continued to make the concealer even tighter. But whatever is hidden in the darkness will eventually come to light. And sure enough, an active pregnancy cannot be hidden forever. And so, I began to count down the months, weeks, and days as the moments slipped by very fast. It was very easy to conceal the pregnancy from Uncle since he had never had to live with females and deal with this kind of challenge before. And so,

I got by for a while. I had no prenatal care the second time around. I never had to see a doctor for any reason. I was strong and healthy.

The moment came in December 1977. I remembered being in the kitchen with my uncle cooking when I felt very uncomfortable in my lower abdomen. I felt something come down in my underwear; it was wet. I rushed out of the kitchen and ran down the hill to the pit toilet and used a piece of newspaper to wipe myself. Oh my God! It was blood, and I was experiencing immense pain in my lower back and my abdomen. What was I going to do now? And it was happening fast. Please help me, oh God, help me. What should I do now? I was trapped, it hurt so badly. "Uncle, uncle," I yelled from inside the pit toilet. "My belly and my back are hurting me so bad, and I am bleeding. I need help. Something is happening to me. Uncle, come now! Help me! It hurt badly; my belly is hurting me badly."

My uncle came running down to the pit toilet where I was, down on my knees, engulfed in pain. Pain so bad I thought I was dying. "What happen to you, pinckney? You sick?" (in Jamaican dialect). He continued, "What, what? When did this start happening?" he asked, as I lay there on the floor of the toilet crying. I could hear the confusion and the horror in Uncle's voice. Then I heard when he said, "Let me call mass...," then he stopped, and for a moment, he left. Then I heard another voice, and it was the voice of a female, one that I recognized, as she came closer. She looked at me and said, "Are you having a baby?" Then she looked at my uncle and said, "Let's get her into the house and in the bed. Send someone quickly to get Nurse. She is having a baby."

My uncle began to stutter, "A baby? I didn't..." Then he was interrupted by this woman. "We have no time to ask any questions, the baby is coming soon. We need Nurse now!" Nurse lived about 20 minutes' walk away from our home, so someone had to go get her. I don't really know who went, but I know I heard yelling, "Call Nurse, call Nurse, call Nurse!" and within what seemed like about 20 minutes, Nurse was there. Thank God, she was calm.

I was placed on my uncle's bed, and within what seemed like about an hour of intense and severe pain, Baby D was born. With no preparation for this baby's arrival, there was a moment of silence, then whisper. I felt like an animal that did not need any medical care or any preparation for the birth of their child. The feeling of shame, guilt, and rejection began to ruin my thoughts. I lay there in the bed and could not look at my baby. I could not hold her. I cried hysterically as Baby Syd looked on.

My uncle paced the floor, loaded with questions that were unanswered. "What? I did not know that she was with a child. She did not look any different. She did not say a word about having a child, and where is this baby going to stay? There is no room for another child. Who will take care of them? I have nothing!" I could not help but hear the questions Uncle was asking, and there was no one to give him the answers. I had no answer for him. The baby was lying next to me in the bed, the old, soiled sheets that were there prior to her arrival, no formula, no bottles, no diapers, no blankets, no wash rags, no soap. I had nothing to use for this brand-new baby. It was customary for newborn babies to breastfeed, and so thank God, because that was the only resource that I had to offer baby D at the moment.

As I lay there in the bed, I began to think about David and how much I needed to reach out to him for some help; at least some money to buy some clothes for Baby D. As I was thinking, Uncle came in and began to ask me questions about my plans for my situation and the future. "By the way, who is the father of this pinckney?" he asked. (This means 'child' in Jamaican dialect) "Am, am, he lived in another town far from here, sir."

"So, you are going to tell him?"

"Yes, sir."

"When?" he asked.

"When I see him, sir."

"Alright!"

My uncle was a cool guy, very mild-mannered and easygoing. So, he was very compassionate towards the situation. As he walked out of the room, I could hear him saying in Jamaican dialect, "Mi nuh know how you going to manage." As I lay there in the bed, I began to think hard. There must be a way out of this. I cannot do this without help. I needed to find some way out of this web of troubles. There had got to be another way out. But dear God, where do I start? I had no education, no skills; I only knew how to make babies.

SELF REFLECTION QUESTIONS

What parts of your story do you still feel pressured to hide, and why?

Where do you notice yourself wearing a "mask" most often—and what would it cost (or free) you to take it off?

Which coping habits help you survive but keep you from healing? What gentler practice could replace one of them this week?

Who are the two or three people you can tell the whole truth to—and what's one sentence you're ready to share with them?

If you named the truth you've been covering up, how might your body, mind, and spirit begin to feel different?

Chapter 5

The Quest for Rescue

"You dog, you surrey, you johncrow, red gal, red slut, you good for nothing. Look at the next-door neighbors' children and how well they are doing." Oh, the shame that I carried, the rejection, the ignorance, and the lack of knowledge.

Not having any idea what to do with my growing baby, knowing nothing about boundaries, how to protect yourself from the opposite sex, how to take care of yourself in terms of hygiene, especially when it relates to the female reproductive organs, your menstrual cycle—what is it? Why is it? Knowledge is power; without knowledge, one will perish or go astray. In the culture of the old days, the male and female sex organs were a secret. It was never mentioned among us. There were no teachings in school about this very important information or topics. It was cultural, the way our parents generally spoke; scolding the children was by name-calling that was degrading and abusive. Oftentimes, you were led to believe that if you were not in a certain group, you were not important. So, for many young people who did not make it into high school, the only way out was farming or becoming a housewife. And so, in some cases, many in our culture will grow up with low self-esteem, while in some cases, some will be strengthened by it. And so, my only way to hide my feeling of rejection and shame was to hide my daughter, not only from myself but also from her siblings and the people I would later come into contact with.

The shame of this pregnancy and the horrifying memory of the delivery had a burden on my conscience that plagued me constantly. *I must get some help*, I pondered in my mind. Maybe I could be able to get these things out of my head, and then maybe some of them could be erased. The thought of facing my family members was horrifying. What would I tell them? How could I even look at their faces? I was a complete failure, I thought. My emotions kept telling me that no one would ever love me and that no one would ever speak anything good about you anymore. As I sat in the bed with both babies in my arms, having nothing to feed them, I suddenly began to speak to myself again, but this time, it was a different conversation. I said to myself, *I did not have these children on my own, so why am I here beating up myself about this situation that does not involve just one person? Regardless of how I got these babies, I did not make them alone. So I needed to do something and do it right away.*

So, the thought came to me that I should go into the town where Baby D's father was living and tell him about the birth of our daughter. I was sure he would be happy, and things would change. Oh, what a brilliant idea, I thought. I had no money and no proper clothes, but I must find my way into Spear Town. The busiest day of Spear Town was usually Saturdays, and so I made the arrangements to go the following Saturday. The days went by quickly, and Saturday arrived. I packed my bags, got Baby D ready, and left Baby Syd with Uncle. What a great blessing Uncle was to us, as I woke up in the morning to catch the 5:00 a.m. bus into Spear Town. We turned down to the gate in the dark and waited for the bus to arrive. Finally, it came, and as we hopped on and I was about to ask to speak to the driver, the driver looked at the conductor and said, "It's ok, let her." By this time, he was familiar with my family situation and had made me his charity case.

As the bus made its way into town on a three-and-a-half-hour ride, excitement and fear boiled in my stomach, wondering what the outcome of this trip would be. Would he be excited, I wondered? Was he working? Would he give me some assistance? At times, I would fall asleep with Baby D in my hand. Thank God she slept also. Finally, we are here! As my heart pounded and cold sweat washed my neck and face, I wondered what I would do if he ignored us. Then where would I go to find money to go back home? What an embarrassment this was going to be for me again.

I got off the bus and made my way to the home, another 25-30 minutes' walk, and as I approached the house, I saw David's cousin. He greeted me and then said, "David is not here; he went to work." "Thank God he's working," I said. I was full of excitement, only thinking that this was going to be a very happy time when I finally placed my eyes on him, thinking that the reasons why he hit me when I was pregnant was because he could not find food or proper shelter for us. And so I hurried into town and stepped inside the store that he was employed, a proud mother. Oh dear, there he was. "David, David!" He looked at me and asked, "What are you doing here?" I said, "The baby…" He said, "I'm working right now." I said, "But I have the baby, and I need money to buy some things." David looked at me and said, "I don't get paid this week, not until next week. Come back next Saturday." I stood there in disbelief, with tears running down my face and snot running down my nose as David walked away.

I sat down on the bench with Baby D in my arms and realized that I had to sit right there until 4:00 p.m. that evening when the bus was ready to go back home. Baby D began to cry, so I took my breast out and began to breastfeed her. At 4:00 p.m., I boarded the bus and went home with my hands empty. But at least I had some hope; David told me to come back next week, and so I was very hopeful. At least it was something to tell Uncle when I got home. It was better than nothing, I thought, as I tried to console myself.

The day went by slowly as I kept looking up to see if David would change his mind and come back to see us. But I realized very quickly that it was just wishful thinking because as the days slowly passed by and my stomach growled from hunger, I realized he was never coming back. Finally, the bus arrived, and we journeyed home with nothing but a promise. There's an old saying that states, "A promise is a comfort to a fool." And boy, did I feel like a fool. The bus pulled up at my stop. As I hopped off with Baby D in my hand and a promise in my head, Uncle headed down the dirt hill to meet us. As he came closer, you could see the look of disappointment on his face. "What happened?" he asked. "Where are the bags you went for?" With shame in my face, I replied, "Oh, David said we came the wrong week, said he won't get paid until next week, so we should come back next Saturday." "What! You mean to tell me that you went all the way to Spear Town for nothing?" I stood there looking in his face, speechless. The week went by fast…

Psalm 118:8 (KJV) states, "It is better to trust in the Lord than to put confidence in man." I had no idea a Bible with these scripture verses existed. But thank God that despite the fact that I did not know God as my personal Lord and Savior, He was right in the midst of my mess, paving the way for me, and so I honored the promises of David and prepared myself for the following Saturday. I looked forward to the following Saturday, as promised. The week went by quickly, and I decided that this time I would go by myself. Thank God for Uncle, who had no problem babysitting. At 5:00 a.m. Saturday morning, I boarded the bus as usual and headed to Spear Town, this time a little concerned that the same incident that happened last Saturday was going to happen again. The ride in was very uncomfortable, just thinking about the outcome and what would be.

We arrived in Spear Town at 9:30 a.m. This time, I got off at the business place where David worked. I was having a panic attack, wondering what the outcome would be today. Would he even miss Baby D? Thinking that last week was probably just a bad day and maybe he was just embarrassed because he had no money, and so I hurried across the street and into the store, a little reassured that today would be a better day.

As I stepped into the store, I recognized one of the workers that were there last Saturday. As I got closer to him, I asked if David was here. He looked at me with a suspicious and sad face and replied, "No, he went out, and I am not sure what time he would be back. I think he went to do a delivery." "So should I wait for him?" I asked. "If you want to, but I don't know how long you would have to wait." I felt a feeling of discomfort in my stomach as if he was not telling me the truth. His answers sounded as though they were rehearsed, but I was still hopeful that David went out and just maybe he would return at some time during the day. After all, he knew that I was coming; he told me to come back today. As the minutes turned into hours was when I really realized that I was lied to. David never returned to the store, and the young man I spoke to that gave me the message shunned me the whole day while I was there waiting. What a fool I was! How could I have been such an idiot? This was definitely a plan. I bet you he was right in that store, working in the back, as I argued in disgust to myself. He doesn't care, neither does he want to see us. What do I do now? Things were certainly not looking good for us. As I boarded my bus to go back home, I was getting angrier as I thought of how cruel this act of selfishness was. He knew that I was coming, and he hid himself from me so as not to face up to his responsibility.

Here I was, the second week in a row, going home to the children empty-handed. My uncle was really going to think that I was nobody. As I continued to argue with myself and got off the bus upon arriving home, I saw my uncle, this time standing in the yard, looking at me walking towards them, and he burst out laughing. "What happened? You went on another wild goose chase today again? Don't you see that this young man is playing games with you?" he said. I answered, "But let him keep on playing me. I have a plan for him. Next Saturday, I am going back again, and if this happens, then I will..." and I stopped talking and went inside the bedroom, covered my face in the sheets, and I began to scream. Tears washed the sheet in my hand. I was overwhelmed with sadness and confusion. I began to think of ways to really avenge myself, and so I decided to pay him another visit, and if he did not come forward with some help for his daughter, I would give him his child. I thought that I could not take care of these two children by myself. It was impossible for me since I was not working, and he certainly was. The following Saturday, I packed my little bag and took off as usual to Spear Town. As I entered the store, I was told that David left for a delivery. I said, "O.K. Thank you!" I waited for my evening bus to arrive. The day ended, and I headed back home with nothing, the third Saturday in a row.

This time, I had nothing but hate, sadness, vengeance, and anger inside my heart. I got home and went to bed. This time, my uncle said nothing. I will go back next Saturday, I said, but this time, it would be the last time I said. The whole week I plotted and came up with a final plan. Saturday morning could not come fast enough for me. I knew that David had an aunt that lived in the upscale part of Spear Town. I also knew that she worked and she was very nice when I met her. I knew that if she knew what was happening to me and the children, she probably would try to help us in some way. But as I was reasoning this out in my head, I kept telling myself that mediation at this point was useless. I believed and had already confirmed it in my mind that I was on my own and that I had to find another way out to help myself monetarily or with any assistance. I realized then that these children, Baby D and Baby Syd, would eventually suffer. If I had to sit and depend on this guy or anyone else, I was going to perish. And so, the more I thought, was the more it became strong in my spirit that I had to give this child to her father so I could find help.

You dog, you red slut, you surrey—these names kept playing in my head, and I believed them to be true. At this point, I had already decided in my mind that I was nobody, and that was final. I didn't really care anymore; we had to live and not die.

The fifth and final Saturday morning came. I packed Baby D's bag with what little she had, and I followed my usual routine and headed off to Spear Town, leaving Baby Syd with Uncle. This time, the journey was long and painful. Tears washed my face, dripping down on Baby D's face as she opened her eyes and looked up at me. I believed that if she could talk, she would ask me what was wrong, why was I crying so hard? The decision that I made began to speak to me in a very real way: "You are not going to see her again." But the stage was set, and I was not going to change my mind. Somehow, someway, he was going to have to help. Then I would get a chance to help myself so I could provide for my children. In an untrained mind, I thought it was going to be that easy. I actually believed that it was going to work. I had it all planned out.

As the bus pulled into Spear Town, I came off and headed to David's job and asked, "Is David here?" "No!" the gentleman replied with a look of disgust on his face. I looked at him with disgust and replied, "Tell him I said thank him!" I began to walk, and I walked for about 45 minutes to David's aunt's home. As I approached her home, her daughter, who was sitting on the doorstep, as I walked up to her, greeted me and smiled, "Oh my, she is so cute!" as she held Baby D in her arms in a gentle and cuddly manner. I saw the love and care in her eyes as she pulled Baby D up to her bosom and kissed her. "Hi, my cousin, what is your name?" she asked. At that moment, I realized that they could do for her more than I could. They had the space to accommodate her, they had food, she would be better off here with this family, and so I popped the big question, "Um, could you watch her for me until I get back? I am going into town; I will be right back." This was a good opportunity to make my getaway. This was just the way I planned it. "Oh, yes, I can! Around what time will you be back?" she asked. "Not too long, I am just going into town to get something from David." "Oh, O.K. Go ahead, I will be right here."

I kissed Baby D with sadness in my heart, knowing that I would not be returning for her. Then I hurried away quickly, thinking this young lady was going to see right through me and changed her mind about watching Baby D, and then I would be caught red-handed. I hurried into town, running and walking, very scared, as I kept looking behind me to see if anyone was following behind me. As the cars on the busy highway passed me by, I turned my face towards the bushes on the sidewalk so as not to be noticed. Oh, dear God, they were coming to get me, and I was going to be arrested. *What if she found out and sends the police to get me? I was going to be arrested*, I kept repeating in my head.

Finally, I made my way into town, and within an hour and a half, the bus arrived. I got on quickly, sat in my seat crunched down, so as not to be noticed. Every time someone looked at me, I began to think that they knew what I did and they are planning to get me arrested. What would I tell the police when they got here? I asked myself. As the bus got closer to home, I began to feel relieved. Finally, I got off at my stop around 8:00 p.m. I looked up, and there was Uncle and Baby Syd standing in the yard waiting for me as I walked up the hill towards them. I was weak in my body, thirsty and hungry, not able to speak, fear taking hold of the very essence of my being. I said to Uncle, "The police are coming to arrest me now!" He replied, "Why?" I said, "I left Baby D in Spear Town with David's cousin, and I am afraid that they are coming after me, and I do not know what to do." Uncle said, "You did what? Where is Baby D?" I said, "I have no money. I went into Spear Town today, and just like the other times, David hid and told his coworkers to tell me he went out to do a delivery. I waited for hours, and he has not returned, and so I decided to leave Baby D with him."

My heart felt as though it was falling through the floor. I could not keep up anymore. *Lord*, I would pray, *please give me strength to make it.* This was harder than I really thought. My uncle was saying very little at this time. As Baby Syd stared in my face with looks of concern, I laid there in the bed, not having any real plan in mind, but just staring at the ceiling. What must I do now? I must have fallen asleep while thinking about this situation. In the middle of the night, I woke up restless and nervous. Must I go back and get my baby? I asked. Was she hungry? Did David get home from work and was he upset? Oh my Lord! I knew that he knew where I lived. Was he going to come and find me, or would he keep her? But what if he gave her away to strangers? Then I would never see her again. I was up all night until daybreak, with pain all over my body. My troubles seemed as though they had multiplied, and instead of me feeling better, I was starting to feel worse, thinking, *Dear Lord, what have I done? Did I make the right decision, or did I create a bigger problem and made things worse?* As the seconds turned into minutes and the minutes turned into days and the days into weeks, I would be keeping watch to see what would happen.

Finally, things began to quiet down, and I decided that I would look for work. But miraculously, on a Sunday evening, I was home when a truck pulled up outside the driveway and a couple walked up into the yard and said hello and asked to see my uncle. Uncle came running out of the kitchen, smiling. "Hello, Cuz, how are you?" They hugged and began to reminisce, talked about how long they haven't seen each other. Then Uncle introduced me to them. These are your cousins, your aunt's daughter and son-in-law who lived in Kingston. They stopped in to say hello. As we met and greeted, I expressed to them how much I needed help, that I was living with my uncle and was not working at the moment. I asked them if they could find me a job in Kingston. "Yes!" she said. "I have a couple of children, and I have no help. My wife would be happy to get some assistance from you for the children." I could not believe what I was hearing. This had to be a miracle. The arrangements were made. They left and promised that they would come back for me when I got my daughter's living arrangements situated. The next day, I left to go to my aunt. Maybe she would be able to watch my daughter for me. After all, she was kind enough to keep us when I was moving to Spear Town for a couple of weeks; now it was only Baby Syd. I didn't think she would have a problem helping out. I knew that the last time I was there with Baby Syd, they adored her.

I packed Baby Syd's belongings and I hurried off to Mt. Roar, where I was warmly welcomed. The reception was warm as usual. I sat with Aunt F and told her the whole situation. With tears flowing down her eyes, she said, "Yes, anything to help you. I will keep her. Don't worry. But why didn't you say something when you were here the first time?" "I just did not want to bore or worry you; you had enough on your hands." I accepted her offer, and we spent the evening together just talking about the old times and all that had happened. She talked about the things that happened to her and her new husband, and then we went off to sleep.

The next morning, we woke up and I had a cup of coffee and headed down to the roadside where I hitchhiked my way back home. I was on a roll; things were looking good. Soon I would be working, and then I would be able to get a place of my own where I could have my children back, and we could be together. Thank you, Lord, for the breakthrough. It's only up from here, or so I thought.

SELF-REFLECTION QUESTIONS:

When life feels unmanageable, who or what do you instinctively reach for—and how has that choice helped or hurt you?

What would "rescue" look like if it came from within you rather than from another person?

Which promises or fantasies have you clung to in hard seasons, and what reality do you need to face to move forward?

Where are you waiting to be saved when a small, courageous step (a call, an appointment, a boundary) could start the change today?

Who are the safe, wise people you can invite into your next chapter—and what specific help will you ask them for?

Chapter 6

Blessing to Disaster

Finally, the weekend arrived, and my cousin's husband came to pick me up in that same truck he had visited us in before. I was on cloud nine; finally, I thought, I would be able to do something productive. I kissed Uncle, got into my cousin's truck, and off we went, heading into the big city. We chatted for a little ways into the city, but the thought of my children haunted me, and I could not shake the feeling of loneliness. Still, I knew I had to find a way out for us. *Soon I will be with them*, I told myself.

The ride was long but comfortable. As I had never gone into Kingston before, I was excited and very curious; I had always heard so much about this great city. It was getting a little dark as we entered Kingston, and the city lighting was beautiful. My cousin-in-law began to show me some of the tourist spots. Then he said that he was going to stop at a famous spot where he was going to get something to eat. I was beside myself. I had never been out to a restaurant before, and so I welcomed the invitation. We went into a place that had bamboo all around it, facing the beautiful blue sea; the restaurant itself sat almost directly on the sand. I was completely lost for words. We ordered our dinner, but I did not order my own drink. My cousin-in-law ordered for me. I sat down to eat, but something strange began to happen to me as I ate. I began to see people in twos. I was in a disorienting daze, and my whole body began to feel weak. I think I passed out.

The next morning, I woke up in bed at my cousin's home. I tried to remember all that had happened to me between having dinner and how I managed to get to my cousin's home, but it was a complete blank. My cousin-in-law did not speak to me about the events of that night. Strangely, he barely spoke to me at all while I was at the home; he completely ignored me. But I knew that night, someone had sex with me. I did not know who, but I felt dirty and was in a very bad state. My underwear was layered with semen, and I realized with a horrifying certainty that I had been drugged and raped. Someone had put something in my drink, but who could I possibly speak to about this violence? No one.

Instead, I began to blame myself. *Who would listen to you? You were only a slut, who deserved what you got. You should have never allowed him to take you into that place with him.* So I kept quiet, because even if I was to tell my story, I had no details to share. I was knocked out. In my own mind, I was nothing more than a drunk.

And so, as I began to get adjusted to this new environment, I started to meet the rest of the family. I pretended as if all was well, but every time I came face to face with my cousin-in-law, I would hang my head down in shame. But the thing that amazed me was that he never acted as if anything at all had happened; he always kept a straight face and acted perfectly normal. I had the great privilege of meeting my aunt and my other cousins. They were Christians, and so I began to go to church with them. At the time, church meant nothing to me. I absolutely did not understand anything that was going on during our times of service. One of my cousins was very mild-mannered and easy-going, but the other one was not so nice. I sat with them and told them about Baby D, and that I would like to find her but I was very scared. One evening we went out to Spear Town, but we all got scared and returned home.

In the process of time, I began to have disagreements with one of my cousins. We got into a fight, and she hit me in my face, which left an open cut. At this point, things were getting really bad, and so I decided to leave and go back home to Uncle's. This was the second time that an opening I thought was going to be a blessing had turned out to be a disaster. There is an old saying that says that not everything that glitters is gold. Even though I had no job and no money, life at Uncle's was much better. I was getting some money for my services in Kingston, but it was not what I expected.

Daniel 1 (KJV) declares that Daniel was taken from his home in Jerusalem at a young age into Babylon among strange people, was forced to eat strange food and worship strange gods, and because he refused to bow to those requests, he was thrown into a burning fiery furnace and into the lion's den. At the time of my journey, I had no idea that I was on a trip for a purpose; after all, I was too busy trying to find stability to even realize what was happening to me. My entire life's concern then was wrapped up in finding rest, and every time I thought I found it, I was disappointed all over again. But deep inside, there was absolutely nothing that was telling me to give up trying to find that rest. So here I am, headed back to base again for the third time around. I went back to Uncle's, spent the night there, and then the next day I went home, but nothing much went on there. I then went on to my grandma's house. The reception was average, thank God.

During this time, I met one of my older brother's girlfriends, Jane. She was very friend-ly. Both of us were basically homeless, and so we began to move about the community together. Jane was an alcoholic, and one bright and beautiful Saturday evening, she invited me to come along with her to a bar, where I stood and watched her drink herself away. At closing time, we decided that we were going home, when it suddenly dawned on us that we had no home to return to. She was drunk, but I was never a drinker, and so I could make a sober decision. Then she said to me, "Let's just go behind this building."

I asked, "Behind the building, where?"

She said to me that we were going to sleep right in this coffee field. I realized then that we had no other choice, and so we hurried over to the back of the bar into the coffee farm, found a rock, and sat on it until daybreak. Genesis 28:10-11 (KJV) says, "And Jacob went out from Beersheba, and went toward Haran. And he lighted upon a certain place, and tarried there all night, because the sun was set; and he took of the stones of that place, and put them for his pillows, and lay down in that place to sleep." He encountered many hardships. This was a rather frightening experience for me. As Jane sat on the rock and snored, it was obvious to me that this was nothing new to her. This was most definitely her norm. The night was dark; the only light was the lights from the bugs, and you could hear them buzz as they came closer and closer to us. *Oh my Lord, I didn't think I could do this.* I was cold. As I tried to pull my shirt down to cover my knees, I could feel bugs crawling up my feet, and there were frogs jumping all around. Oh, oh, oh... There was a voice in my head saying, "Run, get up and run," but I stayed brave until daybreak, before anyone noticed us. We went to my brother and grandmother and pretended as if we had spent the night at a friend's home.

Later that day, Jane headed off to the bar again. This time I decided not to stay out late with her. I left and went to grandma's, but when I got there, everyone was already sleeping. And so my next and only choice was to go into the coffee farm behind the kitchen, this time all alone. I headed into the coffee farm and found a large rock and sat there. As I sat there, I heard all sorts of walking, bugs buzzing, and at times I heard people talking amongst themselves as they walked home. *Oh, should I go out to them and ask for help? No, they will only have the worst to say about me.* The voice in my head ran on—*you Johncrow, you slut dog.* I just knew that anyone who saw me in this coffee farm would only look at me as the names I was called: the dog that hopped from place to place. And how would I be able to explain to them otherwise?

Finally, daybreak came. It felt as though I had been sitting in that coffee farm for two nights and had not slept, but there was no time for a pity party. I got out early and headed to Mount Roar to see Baby Syd. Upon arriving, via my usual way of hitchhiking, they were happy to see me but had nothing to offer, as usual. By this time, in my mind, I had already forgotten about Baby D. I greeted everyone, took a bath outside, and took a nap. I spent the night there but left out the next morning. I said to myself that probably if I stopped by grandma's, someone might miraculously do something for me or make a suggestion that would help at this time. I got into the town my usual way and headed off to grandma's again. Upon arrival, she greeted me and asked what I was doing with myself. I told her that I was looking for work. She sighed, kissed her teeth, and said, "Good luck." She gave me something to eat, then I headed out, this time walking into town with nowhere specifically in mind, but just to walk. I had run out of ideas, run out of trying, run out of places to go, so I decided to let me just go into town and see what would happen.

SELF-REFLECTION QUESTIONS:

Recall a time something that felt like a blessing began to unravel—what were the first hairline cracks you noticed?

What inner warnings (gut checks, boundaries, values) did you override to keep the "blessing" alive?

When the fallout came, how did you protect yourself—and who or what steadied you?

What hard truth did the disaster reveal about you, them, or the situation—and how will that truth shape your next choices?

If you could meet your earlier self at the first red flag, what single, brave step would you tell them to take right then?

Chapter 7

The Englishman: New Beginnings

As I began to walk, I heard a vehicle coming behind me from around the corner. I stopped, turned around, and began to wait for the vehicle to come into view, hoping someone would give me a ride. My feet were very tired. As the vehicle came around where I could see it, I noticed that it was a brand-new car—a black one. I didn't know the model at the time; I later found out that it was a Cortina. As it approached me, I stretched my hand out, waved, and said, "Beg you a ride, sar?" in my Jamaican patois.

My heart stopped as the car stopped. I ran over to the car and said, "Sir, could you give me a ride?"

"Where are you going?" he said with an English accent.

"Down the town, sar," I replied.

"Come in," he said.

As I got in, he asked me what my name was.

"Precious, sar," I replied.

He said, "My name is Mordecai." Then I said to him, "Sir, I am looking for a job. Do you know anyone that is looking for anyone to work?"

"Yes, Daughta, as a matter of fact, I am a returning resident from England. My wife and I and the children remigrated here two years ago after living in England for several years, but my wife did not like it here in Jamaica. She said she could not handle the mosquitoes, so she left me and went back home to England with the children. I am all alone and need someone to wash, cook, and clean for me, as I don't know how to do those things."

"Yes, yes, yes! Please, sar, I can cook and wash. Can you hire me?"

"Yes, I will."

And as we were talking, I looked up and realized that I was already at my destination. As he stopped to let me out, I began to say, "I thought...," and then he said, "You see this clock right here? Meet me right here Wednesday morning at 8:00 a.m. so we can discuss the job."

As I got out of the car reluctantly, the feeling of sadness came over me, and I began to realize that this was not real. He was lying. This was just a way to get rid of me. I didn't believe that he would come back for me. My mind drifted to Esther, who was called for such a time as Israel's trials. God needed a woman to intercede for them, and so Queen Vashti was demoted so God could use Esther to deliver His people. Emphasis is placed on Esther 1:1 (KJV): "Now it came to pass in the days of Ahasuerus, (this is Ahasuerus which reigned, from India even unto Ethiopia, over an hundred and seven and twenty provinces)."

I hurried to Mt. Roar, where I spent the next two nights with Baby Syd as I told them about this gentleman whom I met. They listened, but you could see the sarcasm in their body language. "Are you sure he is coming back to meet you?" my aunt interrupted.

"Yes," I said with some doubt in my voice. "Well, we will see."

That Thursday, I could not sleep. I stayed up all night wondering if this man was for real or if it was just another empty promise like the rest. What a fool I was to really believe that he chose me of all the young ladies that lived in this community—young ladies who went to school and graduated, young ladies who had their teeth in their mouth. By this time, I had three teeth missing in the upper front row, and I was not well-groomed, as I did not have proper clothes with which to attire myself. Why me? But anyway, knowing nothing about faith or hope, I headed out to town and got to the clock about 6:00 p.m., which was actually two hours before the time that he told me to be there. I got there and I waited as I paced the ground. Every time a car passed, I would come around the corner, and I got nervous. By 7:30, I said to myself, *I knew that this was just another lie. I was fooled again; nothing that I did made any sense.* As I was there regretting even meeting this man, I heard a horn beep, and a voice said, "Daughta!!"

I looked up and said, "Oh my gosh, it's him! The same English man!" He was here! I began to smile while covering my mouth.

"Come on, Daughta, hurry, hurry, get in," he beckoned. I hopped in real fast.

As Mordecai took off through town, "Sorry to be late," he apologized.

"It's alright, sar," I replied, "Me nuh have no weh else to go, sar," as I blushed. The ride was about fifteen minutes long, then he slowed down, made a right turn onto a quiet street, and I looked up upon a hill and I noticed a house as though it was a mansion. He turned into the driveway and said we were here. I turned around speechless then asked, "Where, sar, up there?"

He said, "Yes, right upon that hill."

How was I going to work in this mansion? I didn't know anything about working for people from abroad. How was I going to communicate? As I began to blush even more, oh no, this was very awkward. But anyways, he got out, and I followed him up to his home. As I entered into his home, I almost fainted. *How could she walk away from all of this?* I thought. *Everything that a woman needed, and more, was right here in this house. Why, why did she leave?* I whispered to myself.

Mordecai invited me in, showed me around, and told me what my duties were. I was speechless. After seeing inside, he took me back out on the verandah (deck) to discuss hours and payment. So, things felt good. I felt at that moment that this was the breakthrough I had been looking for. I did not know then, but I do know now, timing is everything. As we discussed salary, $350 per week, it sounded very reasonable, and I would live at the home, and then I would go home on weekends. Wherever home was, I did not know, but Baby Syd was in Mount Roar, so that was where I intended to go until I got things on track and on the right schedule. At the end of the discussion, I figured that all the bases were covered. Mordecai decided that it was time to go. The arrangement was now made for me to go home and return on Monday morning to start working, which was fine with me. I would have loved it if he had allowed me to stay at that moment, but it was not possible. Wednesday was fine. Mordecai dropped me off in town. This was a great feeling, driving in the front seat of a new car with a returning resident from England. This was an awesome and exciting moment in the history of my life. I made my way home, skipping and jumping around like a child. This was absolutely the best news I had heard since I had been on my journey, and it was actually different. This time I spoke with someone who appeared to be sincere. I got back home and shared the good news with Aunty, who was very excited. The weekend went by quickly as I got myself prepared for my new job. Monday morning came, and for the first time, I took the bus into town and paid my fare.

This time I did not have to hitchhike. I got into town, took another bus halfway up, and then I walked the rest of the way to Mordecai's home.

As I arrived, Mordecai was in the garage working on his car. He looked up at me with a pleasant smile on his face. "Good morning, Daughta, how are you this morning?"

"Alright, sar (sir)," I replied.

"Glad you made it," he replied.

"Yes, sar (sir)," as he instructed me to go up. "The door is open, just go in and do your thing," he said.

"OK, sar (sir)."

There was no way I was going to remember everything. I began to bargain with myself. How was I going to know how to use the vacuum cleaner? I had never used one before. And the iron was an electric iron—where do I put it, or how would I turn it on? I asked myself. Then he called me in and said you can begin by making some breakfast; everything is in the kitchen for you. "Yes, sir." I walked in and placed my bag in the bedroom that he told me to stay in. As I walked in the room, I put my bag on the carpeted floor. I had never walked on carpet before. I pushed my palm on the mattress of the bed and was shocked that the bed was rather soft; it was not banana trash or (*kiah*). Oh my, how would I get adjusted to all this new way of living after being homeless for so long? As I entered the kitchen, my biggest challenge faced me, which was the stove. Was I supposed to make breakfast on this stove? Where and how was I going to use this? I began to feel as if this was going to happen again. He was going to find out that I could not use this equipment, and I would be fired and replaced again.

Fear got a hold of me. I began to speak to myself: *No way was I going to let this job get away from me. I was going to find a way to do this job. I would prove today to anyone who thought I was a dog, a johncrow, or a slut, that I was not! I must do this job to the very best of my ability.* I said to me. Might I remind everyone, I knew how to do the job manually, for this was the only way I knew how to, but I had no idea how to use the machines to make working easier. I was only used to getting down on my knees and scrubbing floors, going out into the woods and picking up wood to make a fire to cook a meal. But now I was being exposed to modern living, and I was determined to learn. With a strong determination and a made-up mind, I walked into the kitchen and looked at the stove. I began to touch different buttons, then I began to turn them. Suddenly I heard click, click, and puff! Fire gushed out from one of the burners. I turned the faucet on, looked under the sink, and got a pot. All of these were brand new to me. Despite the fact that I lived temporarily in some nice homes, there was none that had this modern equipment in them such as this one. That morning, I made dumplings with codfish, callaloo, and green bananas. As I was finished, I stepped outside and called Mordecai. "The food is ready, sir."

"OK, Daughta, be there in a minute."

As I stepped back inside, I headed to the bedroom and into the bathroom. I remembered the hamper with the dirty clothes. I brought them outside to the washroom, collected water, and began to wash his clothes manually. At the end of the washing, I hung the clothes on the outside line, and as I hung them, the breeze from the wind began to blow them back and forth. Oh, I felt so important. As I turned my head towards the garage and looked down at Mordecai, I was just on time to see him looking up with a smile of approval on his face. Yes, yes, yes, he was happy!

Then he called up to me, "I am coming up now. Is the food ready, Daughta?"

"Yes, sir," as I hurried inside and dished his food out. As soon as I was done, Mordecai walked in. I placed his serving on the table. As he started to eat, I became nervous and started to worry, *What if it was not tasty? He was going to let me go.* As I stood there and waited, I heard, "Yum, yum, this is good. Who taught you how to cook, Daughta?"

"My mother, sir."

"This is good," he continued. "Did you eat?"

"No, sir," I said.

"OK, stop and join me. Take a break."

My face, I imagine, was probably red, but I was sure it was, and my palms are now sweating. Sit down to eat dinner with him? How was I going to do that? I had never really been invited out to dinner, and he was using a knife and a fork. I had never used a knife and fork. How embarrassing was this going to be for me? Terribly embarrassing! I dished a plate with a very small amount, knowing that I could not use the knife and fork, and also that I had some poor teeth in my mouth. I had to eat slowly so as not to be embarrassed. I sat at the table with Mordecai, and I began to eat my meal. The moment was awkward, but I managed to pull through. Mordecai finished his meal and got up. "Thank you, Daughta, very good. I want you to look in the fridge and take out some chicken to fix for supper, you hear."

"Yes, sir!"

Mordecai left and went back to his work at the garage as I continued my washing. Then I came in and began working on the floors where there was no carpet. As it got closer to the evening, I began to prepare dinner. At the completion of dinner, Mordecai was already inside. He complimented me on how lovely the house smelled and the clothes hanging outside on the line. "I had no idea you were that helpful." Supper time came, and dinner was served. We ate and cleaned up. Mordecai then went into his den where he had his guitar. He turned his music on and began to play his guitar. As I left the kitchen to go into my room, he beckoned, "Would you like to join me, Daughta?"

"Yes, sir," as I sat in the sofa and watched him play and listened to music. It was an evening of pleasantness, calm, peace, and tranquility. It felt so cozy and homey that I began to dread going home on the weekend. Mordecai looked at me and said, "OK, time to turn in, see you in the morning," as he went to his room. That night I slept like a baby.

Daybreak, I was up bright and early. I went into the kitchen and began breakfast. I started after cleaning the kitchen. About 9:00 a.m., Mordecai came out. "Daughta, why are you up so early?"

"I had some more things that I needed to finish, sir, and I was not used to sleeping late, sir."

Mordecai ate breakfast and headed off to the garage to work on his cars. About two hours later, he came up and said, "Daughta, would you like to go to the market with me? Today is market day, and I would like to pick up a few little items." Oh no, I don't have any clothes to wear. How could I go out to the market looking the way I did? I had nothing that was proper.

"Yes, sir! I would love to go, but I do not have anything to wear, sir."

"Oh, come on, Daughta, there is nothing wrong with what you have on. Come on, we are only going to the market."

With my heart pounding and a feeling of joy flooding my whole being, I began to think, *I cannot believe this was really happening. I was really going to town with this man who was a dignitary. What if someone in town saw me with him and may tell him about me? What would I do?* Anyways, I got in the car, and away we went, off to market. As we got into town, we saw some of the familiar faces looking at us and asking questions. "What are you doing with him?"

I replied, "I am working for him, and I came to pick up some things in the market for the house."

"For the house? What do you mean for the house?"

"Yes, he ran out of a couple of things, and I came to pick up some groceries and so."

Oh my, I just could not help but feel important with a little bit of pride filling up into my heart.

"You mean, you are living at his house?"

"Yes, I stay with him during the week and go home on weekends," I replied. So they asked where his wife was. I replied, "Oh, I never met her, but I understand that she did not like Jamaica, and so she went back to England."

"What! She is not coming back?"

"Oh, I don't know. I'm just the helper."

As we walked through the marketplace, I couldn't help but feel as though I was an English girl too. All eyes were on Mordecai, and everyone was asking him to purchase something from their stall. After about an hour or so, we returned home and put away the items, when Mordecai said, "Daughta, then tell me about yourself." Oh no, no, this was it. I was out of here. Oh, he was really going to see right through me. He was going to find out that I was a slut and I was a failure that already had two children by two different men. What could I tell him as the memory of Baby D's delivery flashed through my head? I almost dropped the bag of groceries on the floor. "OK, sar," I said, trembling in my voice as tears began to flow down my cheeks.

Mordecai looked at me and said, "Oh, Daughta, why are you crying? It's that bad, uh? OK, I tell you what, when you are comfortable, then we will talk." Then he began to tell me about his wife and children. As he talked about his wife and children, I got up the courage to talk to him. I told him everything about me, except Baby D. The shame and the memory of the delivery, the pain I felt in the toilet, the fact that I was forced to take her to her cousin in Spear Town, and the fact that I was still afraid they were still looking for me to arrest me, made me keep that portion of my history from him. I thought that if I did not talk about her or tell anyone about her, everything would go away.

Everything went well for the evening and for the rest of the week. Finally, Friday arrived, and I am saddened by the fact that I had to leave, but I followed the plans that were in place. Mordecai gave me my salary, $350 for the week, and he drove me into town. I caught the bus and headed off to home in Spear Town. As I was on the bus going into Spear Town, the memory of Baby D began to haunt me. How could I get her back? I wondered if I could go back for her. Would they hurt me? I got home and sat with my aunt and told her the good news about my week. Baby Syd was very happy to see me, but someone was missing. Aunty encouraged me that she was with her father and grandparents; she was fine. The weekend went well. Monday morning, I headed back out to work. This time, my boss picked me up in the town. The workweek went very well. But Friday, as I packed my bags to go home, I sat on the deck (verandah) waiting for Mordecai to take me into town.

As he came out of the house, he looked at me. I thought I was in trouble or something. He said, "Daughta, would you like to make love to me?"

I had no words in my mind or anywhere to answer him. I hung my head down and could not look up. I had no idea that this man would even come close to a nobody like me. Was he drunk? Did he really know who he was talking to? At this time, he realized that I was embarrassed, and so he changed the subject and said, "Oh, by the way, when you are coming back this weekend, you could bring your daughter, and you don't have to go home on weekends anymore." Oh, OK, this was not happening. I could not believe he was saying this to me. "OK, sir," as I got into the car and he took me into town. I went home. Monday morning, I returned with Baby Syd.

As I continued my employment with Mordecai, we became very close, and a relationship developed which was more than just employer and employee. We became lovers, which felt very good, as he began to take care of me. First, he took me to the dentist and corrected my broken teeth and the ones that had fallen out. Then he took me to the hairdresser and got my hair done. Then he took me to the clothes store and bought me clothes. I felt as though I was a princess in waiting.

We became very close, but something was very wrong with this picture because as the days went by, I would see the letters that came to Mordecai from his wife, asking him when was he coming home and telling him about the children. I would begin to feel very bad inside. This man, though very nice to me, was not my husband. He belonged to someone else, and so I could not feel too at home. As we got closer, Mordecai began to take me out to the resorts to different dances and balls. We would go to the beach on Sundays and on holidays. Then finally, Mordecai popped the question: "Do you want to marry me?" I was not surprised. I was not happy; I was just sad. I wished he was single, but no, I cannot. Your wife and children in England needed you. But I did not say it to Mordecai. I pretended as if I was not quite ready.

"Let us go to England," Mordecai said.

"No!" I replied, "Your wife is there, that would not be right. Let me go to Canada instead and visit my uncle, then when I return, we will go to England." Mordecai agreed.

We began to make plans on how to make money to start a business and expand his garage. In the meantime, I became very close to my mother and brothers and sisters. Mordecai had a van that held ten passengers. We came up with the idea to use it as a taxi to generate extra funds, and we did. We would taxi from the market in town into different towns. Weekends were our busiest day, in which we would be on the road. All day, business was very good. I would bring food up to the family and took them back and forth to town, and wherever they wanted to go.

But in the process of time, things changed, as it was time for me to travel to Canada. Oh my! I knew for a fact that I would not be returning to Mordecai because he had a wife and children, and it was wrong to get involved between a wife and her husband. But I could not tell him my plans. Oh, how I wished that he was single, but he was not. I knew my intention was not to get between this family. I went there to do a job, and this thing just happened. I was so grateful, but I had to go and not return, to get away from this very kind man and this double life. I knew at that time that life was looking very good for me; I was having a good time. I was living in a very big house with all that I needed as a woman. There was nothing lacking. Everything that I ever needed was at my disposal: the house, the car, the pampering being given to me by true love without hypocrisy. I was being swept off my feet by a prince. Many people in the community were now looking up to me and were now beginning to acknowledge me. My family was very receptive and was visiting me, and so all was well.

For how do you know that sometimes when God has a mandate upon your life, He does not want you to get too comfortable? He will cause you to rest a little while and then interrupt your rest for His purpose, and His purpose alone.

Isaiah 44:23, 45:8 (KJV) tells us that God used a Persian king (Gentile) to deliver the Jews, His chosen, peculiar people back into their homeland, Israel, for a purpose. So, it was not unusual for God to use anyone to push you into your destiny. This man was a married man, but I strongly believed today that he was used as a vehicle to push me further into my destiny.

I had never told Mordecai about Baby D. But one beautiful Sunday evening, as Mordecai and I sat on the deck talking and laughing, we received an unexpected visitor. She was one of the very important young ladies of the community. As she came closer to the home, we were very surprised as we did not expect her. She approached us and greeted us: very pleasant, very well-dressed, and well-spoken. She was the wife of a well-known police officer and a teacher by profession herself. She was considered a dignitary and a woman of great influence. Oh, my heart skipped a beat as cold sweat began to pour off my face. I began to shake, and it was very obvious that I was nervous. But the portion of the scripture that I did not know at the time declared that who God blessed, no man can ever curse. Numbers 23:8 (KJV): "How shall I curse, whom God hath not cursed? Or how shall I defy, whom the Lord hath not defied?" Mordecai was an ordained vessel, though he had a wife in England. He was placed there in Jamaica to push me into my destiny.

As I was asked to be excused, I got up and went inside. I could hear my heart beating through my clothes. They were sitting on the deck for almost an hour and a half. Then Mordecai came in and called, "Dauhta?"

"Yes!" I replied.

"Come on, sit down. Yes, she was here to talk about you, and she really had nothing good to say. Where is your other daughter?"

As I began to cry, *Oh, you slut*, I began to hear the replay in my head. *I told you, you were no good, look at what you did. You had no preparation, and you banned your pregnancy and hid it from everyone. You are no good!* As I stood there with tears in my eyes wondering what to say, he said, "Don't cry, I understand. As a matter of fact, I just let her have it. I told her it was none of her business and that I did not want to talk about you and what happened to you. I love you, and I respect your privacy. Come on, where were we before?"

"What do you mean?" I asked.

"What we were talking about before that woman interrupted us. I think this calls for a laugh," as we burst out laughing.

What compassion! I had never experienced such love in my life until now. The date was set and finalized for me to leave for Canada. The next two weeks, Mordecai cautioned me and asked me not to change my mind about coming back home. "I will be here, right here, Daughta, waiting for you. Please don't mess things up," he said.

"OK," I replied.

On Monday morning, we went up into the hills; we drove his Land Rover. All was well. As we were returning home, we picked up a couple of passengers. As we made our way back into town, we took a shortcut to get us in faster. When the Land Rover hit a pothole, it suddenly began to tilt to the passenger side. And before I could say anything, it turned over and went over the sidewalk and rolled onto the side. Praise God, a big tree was on the bank, and as it began to roll, it was intercepted by the tree. As we all began to crawl out, we began to check if anyone was hurt. Thank God all four of us, including passengers, came out alive and without a scratch.

As people began to gather at the scene, they all got together and pushed the Land Rover back on its four wheels. Surprisingly, the van came out without a scratch; all was intact. "Are you OK, Daughta?" Mordecai asked.

"Yes, everyone is fine." We all took a minute to thank God. Mordecai got back in, and we went home.

"What a day," he stated. "Maybe this is a sign that you should not travel. I cannot believe that G.B. (he called his van) let me down the way it did. I am still a little shaky," he chuckled. "Are you sure you are OK, Daughta? Anywhere hurt?"

"No, sir," I replied, "I'm alright." We got home from a hard day and retired to bed, feeling very blessed that we escaped that accident without injuries.

The days went by fast, and it was getting very close to my traveling date. As Mordecai began to express sadness, he talked about how much he was going to miss me. I went around visiting some friends and relatives and said my goodbyes. Baby Syd, who was still staying with us, was taken back to Aunty in Mount Roar. That was one of the hardest goodbyes that I had to do, knowing that it was possible that I might not return back to Jamaica, at least not anytime soon. Finally, the day came. Mordecai drove me into the Montego Bay airport and watched as I boarded Air Canada and took off. It was a very sad, sad day. I cried all the way into Canada. As I sat there, I started to ponder on my beloved mother, and I honor her for all that she did and all that she could not do for her children. As the fourth child of twelve, I witnessed her walk as a single mother and say she did the best she could until God sent her a helpmate. Although I was nervous and fearful of the unknown that lies ahead, I had to trust God's plans for my destiny.

SELF-REFLECTION QUESTIONS:

When you've stepped into a new beginning, how did you know you were truly ready—and not just escaping the old?

What green flags do you look for that tell you a new person or path is safe to trust?

Which boundaries will you carry into your next season so your hope stays protected?

How do you honor who you are (culture, values, faith) while opening up to someone different from you?

Who are the wise voices you'll invite to speak into your fresh start—and what do you need from them?

Chapter 8

A New Beginning in Canada

The Grass is Not Greener on the Other Side

Oh, she spoke with a beautiful accent. Oh, look at her clothes; they were so pretty, and her shoes, oh my, look at all the money she had in her purse. And she was being treated like royalty. She could not come into the kitchen; everything had to be served to her, on a platter. Everyone honored her and was very excited whenever she was here. My, my, she was well loved. I wished I could be just like her; she was very pretty and stuttered when she spoke. She brought lots of clothes and shoes whenever she visited, and it was a happy time. Oh, how I wished I could be just like her and someday go with her back to America. I would like to be a nurse just like her.

She, my aunt Lori, represented the future I craved—a clean slate far away from the complicated life I was leaving behind. The truth was, my departure from Jamaica was not just a journey toward a dream; it was also an escape. The tumultuous affair with Mordecai, as kind as he had been, was a dead end, a double life that gnawed at my conscience. I had to get away, and the vision of my aunt was the lifeline I clung to. I would look in the mirror every day and admire the fact that I looked like this woman, or so I thought. I would pout my lips, twist and turn them like hers, and pretend to speak just like her. Oh, if only she would know how much I loved and admired her. But I don't think she realized this. One day, maybe I would be just like her. Maybe I would be rich, living in America, and would be able to speak just like her. My whole life I aspired to be just like her.

As Air Canada lifted off the ground, a voice in my head said, "Finally you are going to be with her, then you would be able to be just like her; you would be rich and pretty." As I sat there thinking, I heard a real voice say to me, "Hello, it is very cold in Canada, and I noticed that you are wearing a short-sleeve shirt and sandals. If I had another jacket, I would let you have this one that I am wearing." As I turned around and faced the voice, I noticed this blue-eyed, handsome gentleman looking at me. He went on to say, "It is very cold in Canada. This must be your first time visiting."

"Oh, yes," I said. "But I am all right," I replied.

"Are you sure?"

"Yes!" I said.

"Do you have someone waiting for you at the airport, because you are going to need someone to bring you a jacket?"

"Yes!" I replied, as I suddenly began to remember that I never notified my uncle to pick me up before leaving Jamaica. Because my English was not the best, as I spoke in a deep, broken Jamaican accent, I did not prolong the conversation. With sincere concern on his face, he said again, "When you get to the airport, if no one is there to get you, I will take you to the Customer Service area, and someone could call your relative for you."

"Thank you," I replied.

After a couple more minutes, a voice came over the intercom: "OK, ladies and gentlemen, we are about to land. Please fasten your seatbelts and prepare for landing." I followed instructions and fastened my seatbelt. Despite the warning from this strange man, I had excitement in my heart. Curiosity was the order of the hour. I was finally going to be landing in Canada, which was the dream of everyone in Jamaica, and so, I was more concerned about seeing what Canada looked like than the weather. As the plane descended, my ears began to clog, and I could barely hear anything or anyone's voice. I turned around to speak, but I couldn't even hear my own voice. As I watched everyone else sitting in their seats, I realized that they were having the same experience as me.

Finally, the plane landed. As we got off, we were instructed by a guard which line to join based on our immigration status. As I was directed to go to the visitors' line, that kind gentleman was instructed to go into another line, and so I lost him. His line moved faster, and he disappeared. Little did I know that I was in for the interrogation of my life. I had heard that you will be checked, but I had no idea it was going to be to that degree. As the immigration officer questioned me, I started to fumble. I was lost for answers and words.

"What is the purpose of your visit, ma'am?"

"To visit relatives, sir."

"When was the last time that your relatives visited Jamaica, ma'am?"

I could not remember, and so I became very nervous.

"Do you have any other relatives living in Canada, ma'am? And if so, what is their address?"

"No, sir!" I answered, fear in my heart as I waited for the next question.

I paid much attention to the officer; he did not smile, and his eyes were staring at me without a blink. Oh, my, maybe this was a bad idea. Finally, after about two hours, he looked at my passport again, and again, and looked at me again, and again, then said, "I am going to grant you a six-week visa." At that moment, I felt as though someone had turned the air conditioner on and cooled me off from 100-degree heat.

"Thank you, sir," I replied. I took my passport and asked, "Where do I go from here now, sir?"

And as he was instructing me, he said, "Where is your jacket?"

"Oh, I don't have one, sir."

"You're going to need one," he replied.

As I approached the exit area, oh, gosh, it was cold. I began to feel the rawness and bitter chill of the cold coming through the glass door. *'Tis serious,* I thought, as I headed towards the exit, looking for my uncle. I went out to the waiting area, and to my amazement, I saw no one who looked familiar. As I looked around the strange place and experienced the strange weather, I began to remember Jamaica, the island in the sun. I began to remember Mordecai and how gentle he was to me. Was this—I began to question myself—what I really wanted? Was I ready for this? I was freezing. People began to stare at me, and I began to feel out of place, lost, and ashamed.

Then I built up the courage, walked over to the information counter, and asked to use their telephone. The kind lady took the number from me and dialed my uncle, then handed me the phone. As I put the phone to my ears, I heard a male voice: "Hello?"

"Uncle James," I said, "I am here."

"Where are you?"

"At the airport!"

"Oh, I didn't know you were coming today. Stay there; I will be there in a minute."

Thank God. I thanked the lady and walked towards the doors.

"Where is your coat?" the lady asked.

As I got to the double doors, I heard a voice, "Pia!" I looked up, and there, my uncle was standing at the front entrance.

"Come here, girl," he said, holding me in his arms. "I had no idea you were coming today. You are cold. Here, here is a coat. Put it on and let's go." We made our way back to his car. Thank God it was warm in there.

The drive home was about twenty minutes. We chit-chatted about what happened at the immigration office until we got home. Inside was warm and cozy, beautiful; the welcome by his wife and daughter was very warm. I ate and retired to bed, since I was very tired. The next morning, my other uncle came over to visit, and we caught up on old times. We talked about the cold climate in comparison to the beautiful sun in Jamaica. I walked around to the deck and looked outside. The sun was shining; it was a beautiful day.

"Hey, Uncle," I said, "It is warm outside; the sun is up."

"Go ahead, beautiful, open the door and step outside."

As I opened the door and stepped outside, I was hit with a gush of cold temperature. Oh-oh, as my face felt like a piece of ice, I stepped back inside and closed the door.

Staying with Aunty and Uncle was great, but I had dreams and aspirations to go to America, where my aunt was. And so, I began to pursue the possibility of going. I would speak to Aunty Jane at least once a week on the telephone, dreaming of being there with her. One month after my visit with Uncle, I broke the news to him, telling him that I would like to go over to America to visit Aunty Jane.

Uncle looked at me and laughed. "Are you crazy?" he replied. "I am a citizen of Canada, and when I tried to cross the border to go into America, they give me a hard time—not wanting me in their country. Girl, do you think they are going to let you into their country with a six-week visitor's visa? Hahaha," he chuckled again.

I stared into his face and replied, "I want to go and try anyway."

The following day, my uncle drove me down to Ottawa, to the Immigration and Naturalization Services. On our way there, he chuckled at my boldness, saying, "Nothing beats a trial but a failure." I was more determined to pursue a visa the more my uncle laughed at me. I arrived at the building within fifteen minutes. My uncle let me off outside while he went to look for parking. I headed up to the floor, where I took a number and waited. My uncle came up and joined me. Finally, my name was called. I got up and walked into the office, where a Caucasian woman with a deep Canadian accent greeted me.

"Hello, have a seat," she said.

As I sat down and thanked her, she asked, "What can I do for you?"

I handed her my passport and told her that I wanted to go visit my aunt and relatives in the United States. She looked at me, then looked at my passport again and said, "Oh, sure, enjoy your stay."

"Ma'am," I said, "is it OK?"

She said, "Yes, enjoy your stay!"

I got up, looked at her, and said, "Thank you." Then I walked out and looked at my uncle, who looked at me and said, "I told you, but you just had to come and find out for yourself."

I didn't answer. I handed him the passport and said, "I got it!"

He said, "What you got? What?"

I said, "I got the visa to go to America."

"Tell me you are kidding!"

"No, I'm not kidding. Here it is."

"Girl, you are one lucky girl. How did you pull that off?"

"I did nothing. She just asked me a few questions, I answered them, and she told me to enjoy my stay." But sometimes in life, anything that comes too easy—watch out: there is a catch behind it.

SELF-REFLECTION QUESTIONS:

What anchors will you put in place (faith, routines, friendships) so homesickness doesn't swallow your hope?

Which parts of your identity are non-negotiable, and where are you willing to adapt so you can belong without losing yourself?

Who will be your "first five" in this new city (a mentor, a friend, a church, a doctor, a work or school contact), and how will you find them?

What small milestones will tell you you're moving from surviving to settling—this month, this season, this year?

Chapter 9

The Journey to the United States

I went home happy as a dove and shared the good news with my relatives, got myself prepared, and called my aunt and brothers. I bought my Greyhound ticket and set sail. I boarded the bus for a 14-hour ride, and my final stop would be Washington, D.C., where my brother would pick me up. The ride was long and tiresome. As we traveled, we came to a complete stop and were instructed by the driver to get our passports and get off. *Thank God! Are we here?* I asked someone.

"No!" she replied. "This is the border. Do you have anything to check—any food or liquor? You have to take them out..." and before she could finish, I said, "No, I don't."

Then she said, "So all you really need then is your IDs."

"IDs, IDs for what?" I asked.

"They just want to make sure that you are who you say you are and not someone else."

I got off, followed the line, and as I handed my IDs to the gentleman, he looked at me and said, "Step inside!"

Oh no, what have I done?

"Have a seat!" he said in a very harsh tone. "Tell me about yourself and who you are going to visit."

I began to get a stomachache. I replied, "I am going to see my aunt and brother in the States, sir."

He said, "I see you are a visitor in Canada?"

"Yes, sir!"

"And you were only granted a six-week visa?"

"Yes, sir!"

Then he said, "What do you have in your bag?"

I said, "My wallet and my notebooks."

He said, "Take out what you have in it!" And as I took out my notebook, he said, "Let me have it! Do you have any other relatives in the States?"

"No, sir!" I replied.

"Were you looking for work in Canada?"

"No, sir!"

"So what is this note for?"

"That is not my note, sir; it belongs to my cousin."

As he searched through my belongings, I began to shake. Suddenly, he went into a room; he was gone for at least twenty minutes. Then he came back and said, "I am going to allow you to spend two weeks in America, and if you stay any time over the two weeks without permission, we will come looking for you." At this point, he began to mark my passport with a pen, and then he handed it to me and said, "Enjoy your stay, ma'am."

I stood there speechless. I had no idea that I was going to encounter another interrogation after my permission was granted by the Canadian Immigration Services. As we boarded the bus and took our seats, I could feel the eyes of everyone looking at me as they called out, "Are you OK?"

"Yes, I am, thank you," I replied.

As I sat down in my seat, I was sure that I was very terrified. I must have fallen right asleep. I must have slept the whole rest of the journey, since the next voice I heard was someone shaking me. "Wake up, wake up!"

I jumped up and realized that we were in the Washington, D.C. bus terminal. I got up in my little blue jacket and afro hairstyle and headed off the bus. As I collected my suitcase and took my last step off the bus, I saw my brother standing on the sidewalk waiting for me.

"Hey girl!" he said. "I see you made it with your dreadlock hairstyle."

I replied, "Yes, I am here!" as he clutched me in his arms and welcomed me. He then picked up my suitcase, held my hands, and said, "Come on, let us go. My wife is at home with the babies waiting for us."

As I stepped outside the bus terminal, the wind was cold against my face, and I got into the car. Within half an hour, we were home. The welcome was very warm. I met my twin nieces, who were in the crib crying. My sister-in-law greeted me and showed me immediately to my room, as we all were tired. "I know you are tired. Go to bed and we will see each other in the morning."

"Thank you!" I replied. And off to sleep I went.

At daybreak, I was up bright and early. My brother was already gone to work, so I was able to spend some time with my sister-in-law and the twin girls. We ate and caught up on some family history as she showed me around the house and the community. In the process of time, a very short time, I began to get homesick. By this time, we had already decided that I would not go back to Canada or Jamaica. My brother decided that he would apply for an extension for me to stay in the country longer. In the meantime, I was getting bored with nothing to do during the daytime or at night, but the same old, same old.

My aunt and I would talk on the phone frequently about my plans. I longed to see her face-to-face. I knew by this time my aunt did not know that I admired her the way I did; therefore, no emphasis was placed on me seeing her. She had no clue that she was one of the people who inspired me to even want to be in America. As time passed, I began to withdraw from my brother and his wife. I was so bored that I stopped socializing or even speaking to them. So my brother spoke to my aunt about the changes he was beginning to see in my attitude. I was becoming withdrawn, not wanting to get out of bed or even to go out shopping with my brother anymore.

On a bright, sunny, and cold Saturday morning, I heard a knock on my bedroom door. I got up slowly and reluctantly to open it, as I mumbled, "What does he want this time?"

"Come on girl, you are out of here."

"What?"

"You are leaving!"

"Leaving to go where?"

"You are going back to Jamaica!"

At first, I began to jump for joy. *Yes, yes, yes!* Then, suddenly, I remembered that I was trying to get away from a triangular relationship. "No, no!" I replied. "I cannot go back there. Why are you sending me back home? I cannot go back there. I do not want to go back out there. I prefer to stay here."

He chuckled. "I tricked you. Your aunt wants you to come up to New York and stay with her."

"Oh, really? That is good news. When do I leave?"

"As soon as you get your things packed, I will take you to the bus and ship you out to her."

I began to skip across the long hallway while gathering my belongings. *Finally*, I thought, *I was going to be with my favorite aunt*. I loved her so much. Now I would be close to her and could be just like her. This was what I always wanted to be—just like her.

Then my brother came back into my room. "Pia?" he said. "I just called my friend in New York. He is a good friend of mine—we used to work together doing bodywork on cars. He said he will come down for you and bring you to Aunty next Saturday. What do you think?" Before I could answer, he continued, "He is a good guy and a good friend of mine, and while you are in New York, he will be able to take you places and show you around. Trust me; you will be in good hands."

I felt a little disappointed, but it made sense, as my aunt did not drive. I figured that this would be a good idea. What was one more week to wait? At least I would have someone to show me around in New York. The week went by pretty fast as I looked forward to living in New York and being with the person I dreamt of being with for so many years. Friday evening came as my brother's friend arrived in a beautiful black Cadillac, trimmed with silver trimmings. The introduction was made, and he welcomed me, as he promised that I was in good hands.

"We are a big family," he said. "I have known your brother for many years, and he has been very good to me. So whatever I can do to return the favor, I am willing to do so. Just say it and it's yours."

He spent the weekend, and Sunday evening, we pulled out, headed towards New York for a seven-hour drive. By this time, having spent two days with him at my brother's house, I was now comfortable with him. We had normal conversations back-to-back. We stopped for bathroom usage and to eat. The ride was very comfortable, and our conversations were very interesting. The long ride flew by so fast that it seemed like it was only an hour or two due to our interesting conversations. I was finally going to get the opportunity to see my aunt.

SELF REFLECTION QUESTIONS:

What are you carrying in your life that won't fit in a suitcase (values, stories, hurt, promises), and what will you lay down to travel lighter?

What is your clear "why" for your new beginning, and how will you remind yourself of it when the road gets hard?

Which boundaries or non-negotiables will protect your dignity as you start over (work, relationships, faith practices)?

How will you measure progress in your first ninety days—three practical wins and one heart win?

Chapter 10

Reuniting with My Aunt in NY

Finally, the big moment arrived; I was at the home that I dreamed of being. As I entered the living room, I saw Aunty standing at the doorway, and my heart flooded as we embraced each other. "Oh my gosh, look at you! Why are you so thin? You need some meat on your bones. Turn around, let me look at you. Is this really you?" she went on. The reunion was ecstatic. "You are finally here!" We went inside holding hands. She showed me to my room, where I would share with my cousin. We sat and talked for a little bit, and then we had something to eat. My brother's friend bid us goodbye, and then we retired to bed since it was getting late. I could not sleep. I was just so excited; I kept wondering, was I having a dream? Was I really in my aunt's home, finally?

I slept like a baby. The next morning, I woke up and greeted my aunt. Breakfast was served. As we enjoyed ourselves, I was able to look around. I observed that New York was so much different from the other cities; it was very busy since we were not far from the train station or subway. I could hear the trains pulling in and out of the subway. Right under the train station and around the subway, there were several little stores and people going to and fro, so it was a much busier city life. I felt a little more at home since this was what I was used to. Things were good for a couple of months, but I was not able to see Aunty that much. She worked at night and during morning hours, so she would go to sleep when I was awake.

On a cold Saturday night, I was called to the phone by my aunty; she said it was for me. "Hello," I said.

"Hi, how are you?" On the other end was my brother's friend. "How are you doing?"

"Who is this?"

"Oh, you forgot already? It's me, man; Jake, your brother's friend."

"Oh, okay, I am alright."

"That's good to hear," he said. "But I am calling to ask you if you would like to go to a movie this evening?"

"Oh yes, of course, I would love to."

"I will be there in a minute," he said.

I hurried and got dressed, and within half an hour, he was there. I was very excited to get out, not only just to see a movie but also to venture out into New York City.

So, we left. It was a very cold night, and the wind was howling like a dog across my ears. We made our way into the city, drove for about half an hour, and I had no idea where I was, as everywhere was beautiful and looked the same. Finally, we pulled up on a quiet street that looked almost like it was full of private clubs from the outside. "Okay, here we are," he said. "Let's go. I hope you enjoy." Since I had never been to a movie theater before, I did not know what a theater looked like or what to expect, but since this gentleman was a friend of my brother, I thought there would be no trouble. As I entered the building and got closer, I began to get suspicious; something just did not look right. I began to feel uncomfortable, but we continued in. At this time, I was not speaking anymore. Then I began to hear music and moaning and groaning. I thought, *Oh, the movie already started*, and so we pushed the door and walked in. As I walked in, I almost fell through the floor. For a moment, I thought I was on an island where people don't wear clothes. There were people lying on what looked like a stage, having live and naked sex. *Oh no, no, no, this was not a movie. These are people engaged in an orgy.*

"Take me home now," I said. "How could you? I am going to call my brother. I thought you were supposed to be his friend. What kind of place is this? This is not a movie; this is a crazy place."

"Sorry, I am sorry. I should've asked you if you wanted to come here, but we could go somewhere else."

"No, take me home! No, thank you!"

As we made a U-turn back out the door, we got into his car and headed for home. On arrival, I got out of his car, slammed the door, and went inside.

"Oh, the movie is over? You are home already?" said my aunt.

"No, I just changed my mind, ma'am."

While I continued to stay with my aunt, Mordecai was writing me letters asking me to come home, but I was determined not to go back to Jamaica, considering the situation with the triangle relationship. Living at Aunty's was a little uncomfortable; it was not what I thought it would be. My cousin and I did not quite see eye to eye on some things, and so it appeared as if my journey was not over; it had just begun. God evidently began to manifest to me that I should not get comfortable there.

Your journey doesn't end here, but in my young and silly mind, I took things seriously and responded to the misunderstandings. I fed into the disagreement that I was having with my cousin. At times, my aunt would try to mediate, but it would not work because it was not supposed to work. According to my plan, I thought being with my aunt was my final destination. She was my American dream. However, God knew this was not my final destination and that His final plans for me were different. I had much more traveling to go through. So I was geared up with my traveling shoes and winter gear because it is not over until God says it's over. Many times, we think that because we have come into a place of our own desire, we then begin to take off our traveling gears and become comfortable, not realizing that God is saying it is not over. You have another couple of miles to go because purpose has not yet been accomplished, little girl. I know that you have no beginning; I know that you are ignorant, but I want to use you as you are for my purpose. I know that you don't understand, and you have no knowledge, and that is why I want to use you. Oh dear Lord, if only I had known then. Despite the fact that I had no background, God said in His word, *1 Corinthians 1:27 KJV, "But God hath chosen the foolish things of the world to confound the wise; and God hath chosen the weak things of the world to confound the things which are mighty."* I am reminded that He alone knows how to use my flaws to do great things for His Kingdom.

On a cold, wintry evening, I took the bus with my cousin to the store. While we were on the bus, I noticed this elderly gentleman looking at me, and as he winked his eyes at me, I then looked away. I got off at my stop with my cousin and took notice that the gentleman got off as well. He came over to me and handed me a piece of paper folded up. As I took it in my hand, he walked away, so I was not able to say anything to him. I opened the paper and noticed that it was a phone number and a note saying, 'Call me please.' I could not understand why this nice-looking gentleman would want me to call him. I didn't know him, and so I was rather curious. That night, as my aunt left for work, I thought my cousin was asleep and tried to use the telephone to call him, but something strange was happening. As I picked up the phone to dial, it made some funny sounds.

I kept on trying for a while, but it just would not go through. I did not realize that the phone was taken off the receiver.

In the morning, my cousin said to me, "Were you trying to use the phone last night?"

"Yes!" I replied.

"Why?" I asked.

"I heard you," she replied.

Okay, since I cannot use the phone, how am I going to reach this gentleman? There must be a reason why he wants me to call him, but how do I get in touch with him? As my heart began to race and cold sweat began to wash my face, I thought, *Oh dear God!*

The next morning on my way to work, I used a pay phone and called the number. It was as though he was waiting by the phone for me to call. "Hello, this is Precious calling. You wanted me to call you?"

"Oh yes, yes, I met you on the bus on Saturday. Oh yes, I am glad you called. My name is Jacob, what is yours?"

"Yes, I am Precious."

"Hi, nice to meet you. By the way, I noticed that you are calling from a payphone. Do you have a number at home?"

"Yes, but I do not know how to use it."

"So is there another way to contact you?"

"No."

"Okay. I would like to get to know you, but if you don't have a number, how can I get in touch with you?"

At the time, I had a couple of days of work with an older lady in the Bronx, so we made arrangements to talk when it was possible from her phone. I left immediately and went back home. The next day, I went to work, and as soon as I got there, I called Jacob and we talked for about half an hour. I explained my situation and status to him. "Can we have dinner?" he asked. "Yes, but how? I cannot come back out once I go in."

On the Saturday of that weekend, we met in a local restaurant and had lunch. Jacob was very nice. He stated that he was single and was looking for someone to be his wife and that if I was not comfortable where I was, I could come and stay with him. At that point, I took his offer with a lot of reservation and concern. *Oh dear, what if he was someone that was looking for someone to exploit?* I spoke with him a couple of times on the phone again. It was not easy. I tried to keep it a secret from my aunt and my cousin. Meanwhile, things were getting a little rough at home. I could not say much to Mordecai in Jamaica, who was calling almost every Saturday since he was the only one that was allowed to call, encouraging me to come home.

Things looked okay as we sat and discussed my situation. Jacob was very sympathetic and offered to keep me safe. I felt very safe. In two weeks, we got married. I had no training in any area to work, and since I'd always wanted to be a nurse, I decided to volunteer at the neighborhood health center in the area. I loved it, and I began to meet new friends and learn new skills. I had always wanted to be a nurse anyway, so this was just so right.

My new friends on the job were very nice and very friendly. I would make Island dishes and take them to work, and they enjoyed them. The time came when one of the employees there had to leave to work at another location. They decided one evening to give her a small party after work. The stage was set. As we sat down and enjoyed a variety of island dishes and American delights, we laughed and we talked. Then, we all decided to use the bathroom. I had to use it, and then everyone else came along. As we sat in the restroom area, one of the employees took a plastic bag out of her purse, and they began to put a white powder up to their faces. As this plastic bag came around to me, I looked at it, shook my head, and said, "No thanks, I don't eat that." As it passed me, I thought nothing of this white powder; I just thought that it was something to eat. Thank God that I later found out that it was drugs. I am giving God the honor and the glory, knowing that if it was not for His grace and His mercies, I would be laid up in a hospital room a drug addict or be dead and gone without God in my soul.

The rest of the evening went well, as we left and went home. As time went on, I noticed that Jacob was beginning to change. He was beginning to show jealous tendencies, not wanting me to talk to any friends, no one, especially my family. My stay at his home was short-lived because I came home one evening and we had a discussion. As I sat down on the sofa, I felt his hand come out of nowhere and slap me in my face. *Oh, oh, oh no!*

"Why did you do that?"

As he began to curse at me, I looked up at him and realized his countenance had changed. It was as if he was a totally different person. *Oh dear God! This was not looking good.* I had to leave. I could not stay here, I thought and said to myself. I didn't know this guy, and I was not going to try to get to know him now. I was leaving.

The next day, he went to work. I packed my suitcase and I took off again. For the second time in my life, I had nowhere to live. I was now working as a nurse's aide in a nursing home, making $3 hourly. I took a bus and headed out to the town. My face was still swollen with a black eye. I was going at this time to 'nowhere city.' As I headed towards the town area, I began to ask questions for a shelter. I was directed to a hotel. I went in and asked what the cost was and was told $125 per night. "Thank you, ma'am. I will be back tonight." And so, I walked the streets during the day, looking into stores until 2:30 p.m. Then, I would board the train to work for a 3-11 p.m. shift. At the end of my shift at 11 p.m., I would then go to the hotel and sleep until 7 a.m. in the morning, take a shower, get dressed for work, and get back on the street until 2:30 p.m. This was my daily routine while I was homeless.

I am reminded of Jesus, when He was also homeless. *Matthew 8:20 (KJV) "And Jesus saith unto him, the foxes have holes, and the birds of the air have nests; but the Son of man hath not where to lay his head."*

SELF-REFLECTION QUESTIONS:

What boundaries will help you honor both gratitude for help and your own growing independence?

How will you contribute to the household (time, chores, bills, emotional support) so the reunion feels mutual, not one-sided?

If old family dynamics resurface, how will you respond differently this time—what's your calm, respectful script?

What rhythms (work, rest, worship, self-care) will you put in place so "starting over" doesn't mean losing yourself?

Chapter 11

Homelessness and Survival

I was homeless and tired, but I refused to give up. The journey was tiresome, but I could not stay here. I had to continue my travel with the hope that I would get some rest soon. As I continued to work in this nursing home, I began to meet people. By this time, I had stopped communicating with my family in Jamaica. First, I had no address and no telephone number, and so, in the process of time, I had lost contact. But I continued keeping hope alive. One of the people I met was a young lady by the name of Rachel; she was very pleasant and very friendly.

I did not know at the time that God used people as vehicles to take you to the destination He wanted you to go for purpose. I became very close to Rachel, whom I began to talk to about my journey. She sympathized and began to invite me to her home, and I began to meet her family. I envied her. I was so jealous. I observed something that was so special; this family was so close-knit. They were people of class and education. School and education were things that were of utmost importance to them. On holidays, they came together, and they would celebrate together. I was hungry for that kind of relationship in my own life, but it appeared at this point that it was too late. But I continued to be her friend and enjoyed the benefits of a close-knit family.

One Christmas, they had a Christmas dinner, and I was invited to join them. Rachel said to me, "My family and I would like you to come and have dinner with us this year, and I am not taking no for an answer."

I was so excited that I said no and pretended that I was invited to go out with someone else. "No, no, nope," she said, "I will not take no for an answer. And by the way, I found a place for you to live; she is a friend of mine, and she rents furnished rooms for $25 per week. It is in walking distance from all the stores, the buses, and the train station."

Before I could answer, she said, "Come on, I'm taking you there right now."

"O.K., no problem," I replied.

Upon arrival at the home, I was blown away by the beauty and the area. The room looked very cozy and comfortable, and so I immediately agreed to take it. Then she said, "I have another surprise for you; my brother will be coming to Christmas dinner, and I would like you to meet him. As a matter of fact, I have already told him about you, and he is looking forward to meeting you."

I stopped and was not surprised. I melancholy said, "O.K., if he's anything like you, Rachel, I am willing to meet him. Just tell me what you want me to do. I have not been successful in that area so far. I keep falling into the wrong hands over and over again."

I carefully looked forward to the invitation, knowing that deep inside, I needed to find someone who was genuine. I felt as though I had been misled, or maybe my expectations were too high. I kept hitting rock bottom in my choices, if I had any.

November came, and as I looked forward to Thanksgiving to be in a family setting, the day finally came. The setting was great. Food was everywhere: turkey, curried goat, oxtail, chicken, jerk pork. For a moment, I thought I was back in the island. As dinnertime approached, the guests began to arrive. I wondered what the evening was going to be like. Was I going to feel out of place? Was I going to interact with this family? Would they like me? I asked myself.

As everyone slowly approached the home, I noted a gentleman came through the door smiling, and with a deep voice, he looked at me and said, "How are you doing?"

"Fine, thank you, sir."

As my friend came over, "Oh, Johnathon, hey, this is my friend, Precious, I was telling you about."

"Oh, it's O.K., we met already."

"Good, so you two can go ahead and get to know each other while I go over here and greet and take everyone's coat."

"No problem," I replied.

I felt so uncomfortable, but I tried to play it off. I was not impressed with his physical appearance at first. He was short and not the most handsome guy on planet Earth. So I didn't say too much, neither did I push any interest. The evening went well, better than I thought. I had no trouble interacting with the diversities, as there were different cultures present there, and so that made it so much more interesting. Finally, the evening came to an end, and everyone was bidding their goodbyes. As I sat there and looked around, I suddenly remembered that I had nowhere to go. I suddenly remembered that I had to go to the hotel and pay my $125 for the night, as the furnished room deal was not finalized as yet. Then I heard a voice, "Precious, would you like to spend the night? Then tomorrow we could go and finalize everything with the room, so you could have a place of your own."

"Thank you, thank you, I will."

As the home emptied out and the entire guest list left, I noticed that Jaybess was still sitting at the table. He looked very tired. "Well, I think I'm going to stay here tonight as I have a long day ahead tomorrow. Good night, guys," as he left the dining area. That night I shared the bedroom with Rachel; I slept very comfortably and was very grateful.

The following day, we left out in pursuit of my furnished room and were very successful. As time went by, I began to look into further education, as I had always wanted to be a nurse. And so, I enrolled in a local nurse's aide class in pursuit of a certificate as a start. While attending classes there, I met Anna, who was exceptionally beautiful, and we shared the same classes together. And we became closer. We began to share our stories. We talked about the desires of making more money. The situation and the experiences that we were encountering were the same. As she began to talk about hardship, she asked, "By the way, would you like to make some extra money?"

"Yes, yes," I replied, "I would love to. Where and what?" I asked.

"I have a part-time job in the city. I will be there tomorrow night. Why don't you come down and see me? I will speak to my boss about you, and you probably could start working right away."

I thought nothing funny, since I was still very naive to the street life. I had no reason to think anything funny.

The following night, I took off by taxi to the place of business that Anna gave me. Upon arrival, I noticed that as I got dropped off, I was dropped off at a club/bar. Still thinking nothing, I opened up the door, and I walked in. The lights were dim, and the music was slow and low. As I looked closer, I noticed that Anna was dancing around the pole, practically naked. "Precious," she said.

"Anna," I replied, "Is that you?"

"Yes, come on over here."

"No, I can't, I have to go," I replied. "I cannot work here." I headed for the door and left. I got into a taxi and I went home speechless. "Is this a go-go club?" I asked.

The following day, I went to school. I saw Anna, who began to apologize for the misunderstanding. I reassured her that all was well and that there was no need to apologize. If that was her way of making extra money, it was fine with me, but I could not do it.

SELF-REFLECTION QUESTIONS:

When life feels unstable, what are your non-negotiables (sleep, safety, food, prayer, journal time) that keep you grounded day to day?

What practical plan could you map for the next 30 days—income, shelter options, transportation, key contacts—if everything fell apart tomorrow?

Whose number would you call first in a crisis, and how can you strengthen that support network now?

What pride or shame do you need to lay down to access available help (programs, churches, shelters, friends)?

What small daily win—however modest—will you commit to so survival slowly shifts into stability?

Chapter 12

Love and Heartbreak

In the process of time, Jaybess, who was in contact with me, kept calling, and we would occasionally go out to dinner. Finally, we began to get closer. I was still a little cautious. My history and testimony were not the greatest, and trust was beginning to become an issue for me. But I was also mindful that I had absolutely nothing to compare my present situation with. In other words, my choices at the time were very limited.

I needed to settle down and get some rest in a real family setting. Oh, how I longed for some rest and for people to call my family, but all I found myself doing was running. Every time I thought *this was it*, I found myself interrupted by some storm again. What if this was just another temporary rest for me?

Finally, Jaybess popped the question: "I really love you and would like you to give up your furnished room and move in with me in Newton. You don't have to worry about working right now. You can get yourself together, take a breather, go to school and finish your nursing career, then move on to do whatever your heart desires."

I was eager to pursue my nursing career, and I believed in my heart that Jaybess was very sincere, so I took his offer. "Yes please, I will," I stated.

The road to your destiny is so paved with potholes, roadblocks, and hurdles that there are times we are blindfolded with swelling promises. We get hurt on the journey, and that causes us so much pain. You have to stop sometimes and ask, "Oh dear God, what is going on? Why can't I make the right decision and get rest?"

Two weeks later, I resigned from my job. I completed my nurse's studies and headed off to Newton with Jaybess. While traveling, I was so sure in my mind that though I needed the help, I was making a big mistake. But I did the best I could to hide my fears and concerns from him. We laughed and chit-chatted our way to our final destination. Finally, about 6:00 P.M., after a two hours' drive, we made it. The scenery was beautiful. He lived in a two-bedroom townhouse apartment, shared by him and his brother. We went in and made ourselves very comfortable. He was a very good housekeeper, so I was spoiled, so to speak, initially. He did everything in the home and made me feel welcome and at home. We had some things in common; we loved the same sports and so we would watch sports together. We would go fishing in the backyard, where the river was beautifully situated. I began to pursue work and did find a job within walking distance of the home, as a nurse's aide in the local nursing home.

Three months into working at this facility, I discovered I was pregnant. The response I got from him during this discovery was not what I expected, but I brushed it away. As I got further into the pregnancy, I noticed that Jaybess, instead of being supportive, began to withdraw. He was beginning to come home from work later and much later in the evenings.

One day after coming home from my night job, I received a telephone call from the rental office. "Hello, ma'am?"

"Yes," I answered.

"May I speak to Jaybess?"

"Oh, he is not home," I answered.

"Who am I speaking to?" the voice replied.

"This is Precious."

"Oh, O.K., your name is on the lease also, so I have permission to speak to you," she continued. "I am calling to find out when will you be bringing a check into the office to catch up on the rent?"

"What?" I replied, "The rent hasn't been paid?"

"No, ma'am. I have your information in front of me, and you are two months in arrears."

"Oh dear, this must be a mistake since he hasn't said anything to me, but I tell you what," I continued, "as soon as he gets home, I will let him know and we will call you back."

"O.K., thank you very much."

About 6:30 P.M., Jaybess came through the door smiling and in a good mood. "Hello, how are you?"

"Good. Guess what? I know that it must be a mistake, but the rental office just called saying that we are two months in arrears on the rent."

"Oh no, I spoke to the lady last week and I took care of everything, but let me call her right now." He called the office and spoke with them, and as it turned out, he did owe. The arrangements were made and taken care of.

I continued to go into work at night. The pregnancy was very difficult; I was experiencing very bad morning sickness, so working nights was good for me. Surprise. One night, I went off to work as usual. He walked me to the door and bid me goodbye. I went off, but during the night, I began to feel sick, to the point of fainting. My supervisor told me that I needed to go home. I could, because I was not far away from home. She sent a co-worker to drop me home, but before I left, I called home and received no answer. I knew that Jaybess was probably sleeping, as he was a hard sleeper. Not feeling well, I gave no thought to the phone call that it was not picked up or even why it was not picked up. I hurried along, got into the car, and took off with my co-worker for a twelve-minute ride.

Upon arrival, I got out of the car, walked up the stairs to the apartment building, got my keys out, and pushed one into the lock. *Oh no.* The inside chain was on.

But why? Why was the chain on? Why would he double-lock the door, knowing that I was at work? I began to bang on the outside of the door. "Jaybess, Jaybess, Jaybess!" I hollered.

Then suddenly, I heard a woman's voice reply, but not to me: "Jaybess, it's Precious. She is at the door. Ah, ah, ah, it's Precious. She's at the door. She is home from work."

"Shhh, what time is it? She is home early?"

"Jaybess, open the door!" I yelled again.

"Just a minute!"

"Open the door! Who is that you are talking to? Open the door!"

Suddenly, he came to the door and opened it. To my amazement and surprise, it was one of our friends who lived right next door.

"What are you doing here?" I yelled. "What are you doing here?"

"I will explain later," she said and walked out the door as I began to cry. "Jaybess, what is she doing here?"

"I don't know what happened, but I can remember that we were having a couple of beers last night, and one thing led to another, and we fell asleep."

Pain and lumps and heat began to go through my heart. Why didn't I follow my instincts? I knew that this was a big mistake; I should have followed my heart. "I knew that I should not have gotten involved with you; now look what happened. I am pregnant again." Then I could hear the voice in my head saying, *'You are just who you are. You are getting just what you deserve. He is treating you as the person that you are. You are just a dog, a nobody.'*

The voice was so strong in my head that I began to scream, ran into the bedroom, lay on the floor, and wept. Jaybess came in and began to apologize: "It's not your fault. Don't blame yourself. It's not your fault. I am sorry. Please forgive me."

Where could I find what was perfect? Who was the right person? Was it Mordecai? Did I make a mistake by not going back to him in Jamaica? But at this point in time, that was indeed the least of my worries, as I had a baby in my womb to think about. So I pulled myself together and shook it off.

Surprise, surprise, surprise. *Could I handle it?* I asked myself. I was so naïve in a strange land, among strange people, a different culture, hoping that maybe I could meet someone who could tell me what to expect, someone who could tell me what the other side of life was like. I was not exposed to a certain lifestyle, and I now know that the hands of God were upon me, even in the midst of terror.

As I continued to be that 'mother-to-be' for the third time around, doing my everyday chores, one beautiful morning, as I was gathering clothes to take to the laundromat, I began to empty out the pockets of Jaybess's pants. I noticed that a packet of funny-looking pills came up in my hands from Jaybess's pocket. I became a little surprised, and I set them on the table. I was never exposed to drugs or pills of any sort, but something was just not right about these pills. Later in the day, I took the pills to my next-door neighbor and asked, "Do you know what these are?"

She looked at me with surprise in her eyes. "Where did you get those?"

"I found them in Jaybess's pockets," I answered.

"Oh, my, I am so sorry!"

"Sorry for what?" I replied.

"Those are speed," she said.

"What is speed?" I asked. At that time, it began to come to me that those were pills that were taken for someone who wanted to stay alert.

"Take them and flush them down the toilet, and don't say a word," she said. I followed her suggestion.

Later on that same week, I continued to do my normal activities. Jaybess came in from work. He came in the bedroom where I was and asked for his pants, and before I could answer, he grabbed me around my neck, pushed his fingers into my nose, and began to cut off my breathing. I could not speak; I struggled and tried to wiggle my way out, but with no success. Finally, he let me go, stared in my face, and said, "I am sorry. I don't know what came over me."

At this time, I realized I had to go. But go where? I was pregnant; my world was coming to an end. How could I fix this? There was no way I could fix this. Who would even listen to me? Or who would even help me? No one! I was finished. I did not realize, neither did I have any idea that this guy's lifestyle was wild and involved the nightlife in New York and more. For as the time slipped by, he started to leave on Friday evenings when he got his paycheck, and I would not see him again until Monday evenings after work. New York was his hangout: drinking and more.

After the birth of my son, Baby Dane, things got worse. Baby Dane was kept in the hospital for an extended time due to some illness. Upon arrival home from the hospital, things got progressively worse. I was instructed to go to the office to seek assistance for my son, when I met a young lady. As we began to share our stories, I realized that we were experiencing similar situations. As we shared information, we planned to relocate and start over again, to better ourselves and our children. She gave me some phone numbers and addresses of places to go for assistance. As we parted ways, she promised to stay in touch.

I thought as I left them that this must be a coincidence, as I encouraged myself and told myself that all would be well. At that moment in time, things did not look very well, but I was motivated to move forward and kept trying. I was also encouraged to know that I could get help, that I could go to school and eventually things would be different, because at that moment I felt as though my whole life had come to an end and there was absolutely no place else to turn.

SELF-REFLECTION QUESTIONS:

What patterns do you notice in the kinds of love you've chosen—and what new pattern would honor you now?

Where did you ignore a whisper (red flag) early on, and how will you listen to it next time?

What boundaries will protect your heart without hardening it (time, access, communication, physical intimacy)?

How will you grieve this loss in a healthy way—rituals, community, therapy, prayer, creative expression?

What does love look like when it's safe, mutual, and consistent—and what are three signs you'll wait for before saying "yes" again?

Chapter 13

A New Beginning—Education and Empowerment

I left the office a little more upbeat and was now looking forward to a change in the right direction. I was now practically raising Baby Dane alone. However, with the help of this young lady whom I had met, she kept her word and stood by me as a family. This came after much struggling and collecting assistance from the government to assist me with my rent and food for Baby Dane. Oh, what a pattern. I continued to be a failure. It did not seem to be working out for me in that department of being able to provide for my children. I knew nothing about being a Christian or knowing how to call upon Him for help. My consolation was strictly tears. I would go to bed at times with some food to eat but found myself unable to eat because of my sadness.

On a Sunday evening, my friend Marion called and invited me to come over. She stated that she had something very important to say to me. I hurried up and went over to my friend's home, very anxious to hear what she had to say. Upon arrival, she was standing outside the doorway. "Hi Precious, how are you?"

"Good, thank you. Is everything alright?"

"Hanging in there. What about you?"

"Ha! Alright, I guess, but let's not talk about that right now. I have a brilliant idea that I want to share with you. Come on in, take a seat. How do you feel about relocating to another city? We could have an opportunity to start all over again; we could move up North, and it is a bigger city with more opportunities to elevate ourselves."

The ideas sounded great, and what did I have to lose since there were so many things I wanted to achieve but it was so difficult getting them done? There were times I would sit and regret ever leaving Jamaica, walking away from the new life I had started with Mordecai. But it wasn't the right way to settle and start a life with a man who had a living wife and children, so I kept dismissing the regrets every time they would come up in my thoughts.

"Let's go," I said. "When do we leave?"

"Not so fast. We have to find a place to move."

Neither of us had a job, so it was easy to pack up and go. We began to make phone calls and found an apartment one hour away north, in a town called Mt. Ebron. My son, Baby Dane, was nine months old when we packed up and headed out. The journey seemed long and hard but finally, we pulled in. My old car, which I thought was going to leave us on the highway, turned out to be very faithful after all. We managed to move into a large two-bedroom apartment. My friend occupied one bedroom, her children occupied the second bedroom, and I occupied the living room, which we turned into a bedroom. I was very satisfied, considering I was with people who would assist me and give me some guidance.

With the help of my friend, I was encouraged to pursue school. I first went to the welfare assistant and got some help for childcare. I began looking for jobs. In the process of time, I moved out of my friend's apartment and into my own one-bedroom apartment and began working. At that point, I enrolled in the local community college to pursue my dreams of becoming a nurse. All seemed well; I finally had a good feeling. My son was in childcare, and I hadn't heard anything from Jaybess. But I was not waiting. I was now enrolled in college as a full-time student, while also working part-time. I would spend many days at school, studying hard, since I did not have an education previously. I was in college, but I was still doing high school courses preparing for my GED certificate. Finally, I sat for my GED certificate, and praise Him! For the very first time, I achieved a high school certificate.

I now began to work hard towards my college credits. Finally, after much study, I was able to take college credits. I was known in this local college as a motivator. I would religiously go to the local library, and I would study long and hard to pass my exams. In the fullness of time, I completed all my general studies, at which point I got a good job at a local hospital, where I worked as a nurse's assistant. I began to meet special people and good friends. As an employee at this hospital, after working there for over a year, you can get tuition reimbursement to further your studies. I was bold enough by this time to put in an application for that benefit, and I was considered. I then transferred my credits to another community college so that I could enroll in their Licensed Practical Nurse program. All was looking well. I enjoyed pursuing my dreams and meeting people who encouraged and motivated me to climb the ladder of success.

SELF-REFLECTION QUESTIONS:

What do you want your education (formal or self-taught) to change about your life in the next 12 months?

What fear or belief has kept you from starting (or finishing), and what new belief will you practice instead?

Which three supports will you put in place—time, money, people—to make learning sustainable?

How will you measure progress beyond grades or certificates (confidence, skills, opportunities, service)?

What empowering identity are you stepping into, and what daily habit will reinforce it?

Chapter 14

Another Love, Another Challenge

While attending County College, I met DeLon, a very charming and attractive gentleman, who opened the door for others and spoke properly, also in college while pursuing his career. I was very impressed with his upbeat mannerisms and his clean-cut appearance. I would come down to the cafeteria during school just to talk with him. Finally, he asked me out on a date. I did not hesitate to say yes. "What were you waiting for?" I said, "I would love to." This guy looked like the picture of energy and life. I just wanted to have some real fun and get away from the hardship that had been haunting me.

Our date was set for Saturday evening. We had dinner and then we went out dancing at a local nightclub. I danced the night away. I did not sit for one moment. I felt like there was nothing else to live for but just dancing that night. At the end of the night, I actually did not want to leave. Baby Dane was at home with a competent babysitter, and I had nothing at that moment to worry about. We left the club and he dropped me off, walked me to the door, and actually opened the door for me. He was very proper, and I felt like a queen.

Following that initial date, we began to date, and as we did so, we began to get serious. DeLon loved to wine and dine and loved to go for long car rides to expensive restaurants, walking in the park; which was very special to me, but I had a secret. The secret was my horrible past, which I was embarrassed about. I would not tell him about my experiences.

I shut that portion of my life out and pretended as if it never existed. One thing I never learned in all my journey thus far was birth control, and so in my excitement and fun times, I was suddenly cut down by my 4th pregnancy. Surprisingly, I was caught off guard. Because of the nausea and morning sickness that I experienced during the early trimester, I was forced to give up school. But I continued to work during the pregnancy. Dane suggested that I needed to move into a bigger apartment, so we began to pursue a bigger living place.

Things were good. The pregnancy was very well; I felt like a queen and was being treated like a queen. There were some signs, though, of control, but I was too happy to even pay attention. As a matter of fact, I loved it because in my warped brain, it was a sign that he loved me. Compliments, compliments, compliments were coming from everyone: I was a beautiful pregnant woman. I gained weight and I glowed in my face and my hair grew long and healthy, and so I was being admired by everyone I came in contact with. Oh, this pregnancy was really a blessing. 'You are beautiful,' and so DeLon was proud, and took me to all his friends and showed me off.

The time came when Baby J decided to be born. I went to the hospital where I was in labor for 9 hours with no success. Finally, I was given a caesarean section. Oh wow! It was a boy and a big one, a very big one. "No wonder she wasn't able to push him out," said the doctor. "Oh he is fat. Look at those thighs," said the nurse. "Let us weigh him and see how much he weighs. Oh my gosh!"

"What?" said the doctor.

"10 pounds 4 ounces!"

Word spread around the hospital about this 10-lb. 4-oz. baby, and I was an employee there, so I was treated with royalty. Department heads were coming to see me. The time came when I was discharged to go home and also to a new apartment; a bigger apartment. Being in a larger apartment now, with more space, was an invitation for DeLon to move in.

DeLon was now beginning to show his true colors. He was jealous, controlling, and passive. Work was now not work anymore; I was now being timed. I must be home at a specific time every day after work. Upon arrival at work, it was religious that as soon as I walked in through the door my supervisor would be calling me: "Precious, telephone."

"Hello," I answered.

"What took you so long to get to the phone, and what doctors are you talking to there?"

I was written up by the hospital for too many telephone calls coming in on the unit. Going to the grocery store or running errands had to be timed. If I said I would be back in a half an hour and did not make it back within that time, I would receive a twisted arm, a pulling of my hair, or a plucking on my ear. The abuse and control became progressively worse. At one instant, I went to an interview, on a very busy main street area. DeLon was with me; he drove me there. Upon arrival there, parking was very limited, and so he allowed me to get off at the entrance while he went to find parking. As I waited for him, I began to walk up the steps to the office. As I got to the top of the floor, I went left instead of right. I turned around to make my way back to the right direction when I heard a voice: "Precious!! Oh my God, what were you doing back there? Who did you meet back there?" He grabbed my arms with Baby J in my hand and began to twist. "Was it a man you went to meet back there? Is that why you couldn't wait for me?" After much interrogation, I gathered myself together, went into my appointment, and we called it a day.

I continued to take care of the children while working. It was rather difficult, but I was managing. One Monday morning, DeLon drove me to drop the children off at the babysitter. We had an argument in the car. Upon arrival to the babysitter's home, he parked outside the driveway, and as I got out from the passenger's side, DeLon got out, insisted that it wasn't the babysitter I was going up to see, and so he began pulling on my hair, then he ripped my shirt off. As he continued to shove and push me, the neighbors began to yell at him through their windows, "Leave her alone, leave her alone!" At which point he looked up and responded to the neighbors, "Mind your business, it is none of your business!"

One of the neighbors yelled, "I am going to call the police!" And as she said that, there was a police car coming around the corner. DeLon got in his car and sped away, leaving me standing on the sidewalk with no shirt and a bleeding lip.

The police officer approached me and asked, "Ma'am, can you tell me what happened?"

"We had an argument, and as I was walking out of the car to go upstairs, he tried to stop me and I would not stop, and so he started to shove and push me."

"Would you like to press charges?"

"No, sir!"

"So are you OK?"

"Yes, sir."

"Where is he now?"

"I don't know, sir."

During this time and this relationship, I had enrolled into school again, still working, and on occasion would go out dancing with DeLon to the club. No one from the opposite sex could look at me or even compliment me. If they did, I would be confronted in an aggressive manner by DeLon, and he would blame me, saying that it was because I was looking at them first. I was not allowed to go anywhere by myself: not the supermarket, not work, and not school. If he didn't drive me, I couldn't go. I was not allowed to have any friends. I loved DeLon and in spite of the abuse that I was getting, I just thought that it was because he loved me. DeLon was very popular and had a great personality, and so I was in love with his popularity and personality.

One evening we went dancing at our favorite club, and as I got into the club, a gentleman standing at the door said, "Hello beautiful, you are very pretty." DeLon who was behind me, grabbed me by my hair and pulled me back outside. "What happened just now?"

"What do you mean?" I replied.

"Were you talking to him?"

"No, he spoke to me and I answered."

DeLon grabbed me by my arms and began twisting them. "I told you that you should not have disrespected me like this." And as I was trying to explain to him what happened, someone interrupted, "DeLon!"

"Yes?"

"I need to say something to you real quick."

"OK, stay right here," DeLon said to me, "I am not finished with you as yet."

"OK," I replied, trembling.

As DeLon walked away, I spotted a taxi that had dropped someone off at the entrance of the club. I ran towards the taxi and shouted, "Taxi, taxi!" As I opened the door and got in I said, "Drive fast!"

"Where are you going?"

"Out of here," I replied.

"No, what is the address?"

"Drive first!"

The taxi took off without DeLon noticing. Upon arrival at home, I got in, buried my head into the bed, and began to weep, when the phone rang.

"Hello," I answered. "Who is this?"

"Precious."

"Yes," I replied.

"How did you get home?" Before I could answer, the phone hung up.

Oh my God, I was in serious trouble. What could I do now? I knew that he was on his way home. What was I going to tell him? This was it; I was finished. There was no way I was going to survive this one. As I was sitting in the room wondering what to do, I heard keys in the door. I sat at the side of the bed waiting for the result.

"How did you get home?" DeLon asked angrily, as he grabbed my hair and lifted me up off the bed. "Woman?" He said, "Did you just disrespect me? Was it your man that took you home?" as he was pushing and bouncing me across the room. DeLon would never directly punch or slap me, because he did not want to leave any marks on me as proof. And so, he continued to squeeze me. I began to think of ways to get away. By this time, the babysitter had already left and the children were in the room sleeping. "I must get out," I whispered, "He is going to hurt me."

I thought of calling the police, but I could not. Suddenly I thought of getting out through the back door and driving to the police station; and so I focused on that. But that was also a very dangerous move to make since DeLon was very strong and mean. But there is a saying that says, 'desperate times call for desperate measures.' And so I had to get out. I began to think about my keys and where they were, and how I could get to them. I began to think in my head which door I was going to get out through to make my getaway. As I got that situated in my head, DeLon began to take something out of his pocket; his keys. As he stepped across the room to put them down, I slipped through the bedroom door, ran into the kitchen, grabbed my keys, opened up the back door leading towards the outside, and into the parking lot.

"Precious, Precious, Precious, come back here, I am talking to you, come back here!"

I headed immediately to my car, not worried about anything. I managed to get inside my car and started it, reversed and then put it in drive. As I proceeded to drive out of the yard unto the street, I saw DeLon standing in front of my car. I was not afraid; I did not care what happened, as I stepped on the gas. I was determined to run him over. I had on my nightgown, my hair was out and flying all over, but I was determined. DeLon jumped out of the way, and I sped off to the local police station. I went in and made a report.

"Where is he, ma'am?"

"At the house, sir!"

"Ok, come on."

As I got to the home, accompanied by the police, I noticed that DeLon's car was gone. The children were still in the house sleeping. The police tried the door but it was locked. So they went to the back of the house and used some kind of instrument and pushed the window open and entered in. Thank God the children were safe. The popular gospel song that entered my mind right now as I was writing is 'If it had not been for the Lord on my side, tell me where would I be? Where would I be? He kept all my enemies away; He gave me sunshine, on a cloudy day. He wrapped me in the cradle of His arms, so that the enemy would do me no harm.' If only I knew those songs during those times, the Lord knows that I would've been singing them. I give honor to my mother who raised 12 children. She was unselfish, in that she shared her womb 108 months to house all of us. Thank you Mother. R. I. P.

"Ma'am, would you like to press charges?"

"No sir," I replied.

DeLon was a heavy marijuana smoker. It was very obvious when he was under the influence. He would laugh and would eat a lot, and go on adventures. He would talk loud and would be very stern with a militant, aggressive tone. The following day DeLon came home. Surprisingly, he did not mention what happened that night. It was as if nothing had happened. One bright weekday morning as we pulled out of the driveway to take Baby J to his doctor's appointment, DeLon began to argue with me, and as I responded he reached over, grabbed the back of my hair and pulled on it. Without even thinking, and with Baby J in my hand, I opened up the driving car door to jump out of it. I was tired, and as I did that, DeLon stepped on the brakes. We survived. What I have learned in my journey is that there are some men who do not appreciate a strong woman. When you think that they should be happy that you are helping, they are offended because you are smart.

While experiencing my troubles with DeLon, one day I received a call, "Hello, who is this?"

"Is this Precious?

"Yes," I replied. "This is Jaybess."

"Who? Oh my gosh, where have you been?"

"Oh, right here."

"Right here where?" I could not help but pick up in his voice that he sounded very low and sad.

"How is Baby Dane?"

"He is good. But what about you? How are you?" I asked.

"Alright, but I need to talk to you."

"OK, I will be glad to meet with you," I went on to say, "But where?" I continued.

"My address is 314 East West south St. Can you come this weekend?"

"OK, I will," I answered.

On the Saturday, I got Baby Dane and Baby J dressed, and took off for an hour drive. Upon arrival to our destination, I met Jaybess, as we greeted each other. He looked different. He invited us to sit down. "How are you?" He said.

"Fine," I replied.

"How is Baby Dane?"

"Fine."

"Oh OK, good," he said, "I have something to talk to you about."

"OK, go ahead."

"I have been staying away because I went to the doctor and they said I am HIV positive, and they want me to get in contact with anyone that I have been involved with sexually in the last 10 years."

Oh no, oh no, I began to hyperventilate. I could not breathe, oh dear, I could not breathe. I felt like I was going to die, as the children sat on my lap staring into my face with their big bubbly eyes. The stare in their faces had a big question sign in their eyes. I got up and decided that I was going home. I didn't want to hear any more of this, this was not happening. How bad could things ever get?

I called DeLon and told him what was happening. I could not believe how supportive he was. "Come home," he replied, "We will just go get tested." That was a great consolation coming from him. "Come home now!" DeLon continued.

"OK!" I got up, grabbed the children, hurried out to the car, locked them into their seats and began to drive. Oh dear God! I could not breathe; I could not even see the road in front of me. How could I see to drive? How was I going to make it back home? It was a long way to go. Suddenly; screech, "Watch where you are going you idiot." As I slowed down I realized that I was going around the corner, but on the wrong side of the road. Oh no, I almost caused an accident. I had to pull over for a minute and get myself together. I pulled over, got a paper bag that was sitting in the car, and began to take deep breaths. Then I pulled off and headed home.

I made it home safely, but a nervous wreck. The next morning I called my doctor and explained to him what had happened. "Calm down," the doctor said, "How old is your son?" I told him. "OK, how old is your last son?" I told him. "Well ma'am, relax, if it makes you feel better, you can go ahead and get tested, but nothing is wrong with you, because if anything was wrong, it would've shown up during your last pregnancy. But here is what you do, take Baby Dane to your pediatrician and get him tested, and if he is ok, then you are too, but if you want to relieve your mind and feel more comfortable, you can come in and we will get you tested."

"Oh, OK, thank you doctor," I replied, "I feel much better now."

I hung up and called the pediatrician. I explained, and as she listened she chuckled, "I can tell you right now that there is nothing to worry about, but to ease your mind, we will get both children tested." This was such good reassurance coming from both doctors, and to make it even much better, DeLon was not concerned about it. The appointments were made for all three of us and we went and had all our physicals and blood work done. The wait was extremely long. As I waited for the results, in my mind I was beginning to exhibit HIV symptoms; night sweats and all kinds of symptoms, and so the three weeks waiting period was unbearable.

But thank God, it was on a weekday morning my telephone rang. "Hello, is this Precious?"

"Yes it is!"

"OK, this is Mavis calling from Doctor Well's office, hang on a moment please."

Pitter, patter, pitter, patter, oh my heart was about to jump through my chest. Cold sweat began to wash my whole body. Finally, "Hello Precious, sorry for keeping you waiting, but everything is fine. Your bloodwork is in and everything is normal."

"Thank you, thank you so very much!"

Two days later the pediatrician called, "Precious, calling to inform you that both your children are fine. The lab results came in today and everything is normal."

"I thank you so much, this is good news."

I was very grateful for such relieving news, but there were so many other problems hanging over my head that I needed to deal with. But as long as there was life, I did not know these sayings then; that 'there is always hope'. Of course, DeLon was not surprised about the results and I realized that he was not concerned, for the same reasons that the doctors were not concerned.

I made my final decision to end this relationship when I began to visit churches, seeking help, advice, and counseling. Finally I went to this church with my children; at the end of the service the altar call was made. I went up with my children as I wept; I could not contain myself. I stood there shaking as I began to pour out my heart to this lady. She held me in her arms and began to pray violently. As I listened, I realized that she was crying also, as she spoke in a different language. At the time I thought she was from another country, and that she was speaking in her native language. At the end of the praying, they took me in a room, took my contact information, and promised to keep in touch with me. I left that church feeling as though I was a brand new person. I ran home with the good news, shared it with DeLon, and to my amazement, his response was insulting. He looked at me and laughed. "I don't have time to waste," he responded.

"But they wanted to talk to us and they invited us to come out to their mid-week service and prayer meetings," I said.

"Oh yeah," DeLon replied, "You must be crazy. I can pray for myself. I don't need them."

I was in a state of confusion, "If the church cannot help, then who can? After all, I thought that that was the right place to be, and they are willing to help us," I continued to argue.

During that time I was beginning to meet friends, of which DeLon was despised. He did not want me to have any friends, but I gathered the courage, with the encouragement of my friends, to resist him, which angered him even more, but I was willing to risk losing this relationship at all cost.

On a Wednesday evening I went out to the church service, bible study and prayer meeting, and as I was sitting in the pew, a lady came out of the office and asked, "Are you Precious?" As she stared me in my face, "Yes ma'am," she said, "OK, there is a gentleman here in the back looking for you." My heart felt as if it stopped. Oh my, he is going to embarrass me. This guy was no respecter of any person; not the police, not the law, not the job, not friends, not family members, and sure enough, not the church. Before I could reply, the woman said, "I will send him in." Well, I thought of course this was the right place for him to be. At least he was here. As I was sitting there looking and waiting for his grand entrance, my mouth dropped as he entered with his eyes red and he was laughing. Oh my gosh, this was not good, he was high, he was smoking. As he came closer, you could smell the stench of weed on him. Oh my gosh, I was so embarrassed, where could I hide my head? By this time, everyone was looking at us.

"I came to get you. Come on, what did I tell you?" Come on son, let's go home," he said to Baby J, as he pulled him out of my hands. Without saying anything to anyone, I hung my head down, held on to Baby Dane and ran out the front door. As I got outside he came right out behind me, "You don't listen, do you? I told you we are not coming here. We don't need to come here," he said. At that time I realized that this was the end of that mess. I didn't think it could have gotten any worse. Something had to be done.

The following weekend, I went and spent the weekend with my girlfriend who stood by me, against him. As I continued to resist DeLon, I began to notice that he was becoming less aggressive. He bought me an engagement ring which I accepted. DeLon was now no longer living with us. I was at this time beginning to put my foot down. I stopped going to the church and was now beginning to go out to the clubs with my friends. I was no longer going to school, but I continued working. I was working two jobs while raising the children. Thank God for aunty Orpah, who stepped in. She took my two boys and began to care for them. I was now hiding from DeLon and would visit clubs Thursday nights through Sunday nights, just dancing away my problems. One night while dancing in the nightclub, gunshots began to fire in every direction. Everyone began to take cover. I dropped to the floor and crawled under a table and missed a bullet just in time.

SELF-REFLECTION QUESTIONS:

When a relationship shifts from ease to effort, what signals tell you it's time to slow down rather than push through?

Which three qualities must a partner demonstrate under stress (not just say) for you to feel safe?

What is your personal "pause protocol" when confusion rises—who do you call, what do you pray/journal, what decision window do you set?

How will you measure repair after a breach—what changes, timelines, and proof will confirm growth versus cycles?

What outcomes would mean you honored yourself in this chapter, even if the romance doesn't last?

Chapter 15

A New Chapter: Marriage in Jamaica

The bass from the club still thumped in my chest, even though I was back in the quiet of my apartment. It was late, maybe 3 or 4 a.m.. That had become my norm. Thursday through Sunday nights had blurred into a frantic escape on the dance floor, a desperate, sweaty attempt to outrun the shadows that clung to me. I didn't drink. I didn't smoke. But dancing? That was my temporary escape. For those few hours, lost in the music, I didn't have to think about the weight I carried, the loneliness, the accumulated pain. But the forgetting was always short-lived. The moment the music stopped and the house lights came up, everything I tried to outrun came crashing back, leaving me feeling even emptier than before.

That night, however, something different cut through the usual post-club exhaustion. A sharp, undeniable worry for my mother, who was back in Jamaica recovering from surgery, pierced through my fatigue. An overwhelming urge, almost a compulsion, propelled me to the phone. I had to hear my brother, Dave's, voice. I had to know she was okay.

The line crackled, then connected. A man's voice answered, but it wasn't Dave's.
"Hello?"
A bit of annoyance, then curiosity. "Who is this?" I asked, my voice sharper than I intended.
"Howard," the voice replied, smooth and impossibly calm.

"Howard? Who are you?" My mind raced with a thousand worst-case scenarios. Was Dave okay?

"I'm Dave's friend," he explained.

In the beat of silence that followed, I didn't know whether to hang up or keep talking. His voice was steady, a low, reassuring hum that somehow disarmed me. And then, out of nowhere, a question I hadn't planned, a question that seemed to spring from a deep, unacknowledged well of profound loneliness and perhaps a reckless flicker of hope, escaped my lips. "Are you married?"

"No," he said, and I could hear the surprise in his tone.

Then another, even more outrageous question tumbled out before I could censor it: "Would you like to come to America?"

He didn't miss a beat. "Yes."

It was wild. Reckless. But I wasn't laughing or joking. A part of my soul I didn't even know was listening needed this stranger to say yes. I needed to believe there was something else out there—a shift, a miracle, a new chapter waiting to be written. It felt as if a heavy, rusted door had just creaked open, revealing a path I hadn't even known I was looking for. He passed the phone to Dave, and the relief of hearing my brother's familiar voice was immense.

"Dave, who is this friend of yours?" I pressed, needing to be sure.

"He's a good friend, Anglore, a really good friend," Dave said, his tone full of genuine warmth. "A nice guy, a very nice guy."

His words were like a lifeline. "Set me up then," I blurted out, the request sounding almost like a plea. "Introduce me." And to my surprise, Dave readily agreed.

When I spoke to Howard again before hanging up, the air between us, across thousands of miles of ocean and telephone wire, was charged with a new and palpable possibility. We agreed to try a long-distance courtship. And so it began.

The phone became an extension of my hand, a conduit to a world of hope I hadn't dared to imagine. Hours upon hours were spent talking, our voices weaving a tapestry of connection that bridged the distance between New Jersey and Jamaica. Letters, filled with our hopes, our dreams, and the mundane details of our separate lives, crisscrossed the ocean. I had only seen a handful of photographs of him, yet I felt an undeniable pull. It was his voice, deep and reassuring. It was the way he listened, truly listened, as I tentatively, cautiously, began to share snippets of my story, my vulnerabilities, my past hurts. I told him about the complicated, traumatic birth of my second daughter, the lack of preparation, the shame and fear I had felt, and he responded not with judgment, but with a gentle, profound understanding that soothed a part of my soul I hadn't realized was so raw and wounded.

He was a police officer in Kingston, a symbol of stability in a world that had, for me, always felt so precarious. He wasn't just stable; he was structured, responsible, and seemed deeply rooted. He even promised to look out for my daughter who lived in Spanish Town, a gesture that meant everything to me. I was thirty-three, a woman who had weathered more storms than I cared to count. He was twenty-one, barely into adulthood, but his words carried a maturity, a warmth, and a gentleness I hadn't felt in years. In those long, late-night conversations, the age difference seemed to fade into insignificance against the backdrop of the powerful connection we were building.

I remember one early conversation where I'd promised to call him back on a specific day. Life, in its usual chaotic way, intervened, and I completely forgot. When we finally reconnected, his voice was tinged with a gentle reproach. "You posted me," he said.
I was utterly confused. "Posted you?"
He explained that in Jamaica, it meant he had waited for my call, unmoving, like a post planted firmly in the ground, for hours on end. He'd been so eager to hear from me, and my forgetfulness had left him feeling stood up and deeply disappointed. His words, instead of angering me, touched a tender spot. It made his interest feel real, tangible. In my mind, I wasn't thinking about green cards or someone trying to use me; I was just a woman, starved for genuine affection and stability, who had stumbled upon a man who seemed to truly care.

Within six short months of that first fateful phone call in late 1988, we were seriously planning our wedding. It seemed crazy, even to me at times. I had never even been in the same room with this man. We had no video chats back then, just voices and a few fuzzy photos. But my heart was tired. My soul was tired. And Howard, with his calm voice and promises of care, felt like a breath of fresh air, like an anchor in a stormy sea.
He sent his suit measurements. I bought everything in the States, caught up in a whirl-wind of hope. My bridal party and I booked our tickets to Jamaica. I was filled with a dizzying mix of excitement—and sheer terror. What if this was all a lie? What if he looked nothing like the photos? What if this was just another crushing disappointment waiting to happen? The "what ifs" chased each other around in my head, a frantic dance of doubt that kept me up at night.

The day I boarded the flight to Jamaica in April 1989, with my two young sons by my side, was a mixture of pure exhilaration and gut-wrenching terror. All the planning, the beautiful dress I'd chosen, the shoes, the hairstyle I'd envisioned—it all felt wonderfully, surreally real. But underneath the excitement, a cold current of anxiety ran deep. As the plane began its descent into Sangster International Airport in Montego Bay, that anxiety reached a fever pitch. My palms were slick, my heart hammering against my ribs like a trapped bird. My brother, Dave, being a police officer himself, had arranged to meet me inside the airport, a small mercy that eased some of my fear.

Then, the moment arrived. As I walked through the arrivals gate, my eyes scanned the waiting crowd, a sea of unfamiliar faces. And then I saw him, Howard. Tall. Handsome. His skin kissed by the Jamaican sun. His eyes, a striking red-maroon, found mine across the bustling terminal and stopped me in my tracks.

"Hi," was all I could whisper when I finally reached him, but it was enough. He looked exactly like his pictures, even better, and the chemistry that had sparked and crackled over the phone was undeniably, thrillingly present. In that single, breathtaking instant, all the letters, all the hours of disembodied conversation, coalesced into this one, solid, overwhelming reality. My stomach did a nervous flip, a sensation so intense I was glad for the distraction of my children, something to hide behind as I navigated this life-altering moment.

The two weeks leading up to the wedding were a whirlwind. There was pre-marital counseling with the pastor, meetings with Howard's family, his friends, even his old high school principal. Everyone I met had nothing but glowing things to say about him. He was, they all said, the best of men, and I was blessed to have found him. Their words wrapped around me like a warm blanket, reinforcing my desperate hope that this, finally, was my safe harbor. I was intimate with him during those weeks; I wasn't saved then, had no church background to guide or restrain me. I was simply a woman, hungry for love and stability, acting on the potent, intoxicating combination of hope and attraction.

This was it, I told myself, my Cinderella story. My very first wedding. And I had poured every ounce of myself into making it perfect. It was a "foreign wedding," as they called it in Jamaica, an event that promised to be the talk of the town, and it lived up to every expectation. I'd handled all the attire from America; Howard had managed all the local arrangements, securing the prized goats for the feast and the perfect venue. My bridal party, a mix of my family and his, looked radiant.

The wedding ceremony took place in a small, humble church nestled in the bustling market square of St. Thomas. Even as I stood at the altar, exchanging my vows, I could hear the vibrant sounds of life happening just outside the doors—vendors shouting, car horns honking. Locals, drawn by the spectacle, pressed their faces to the windows, curious about the American woman marrying their hometown hero. The reception was held at his uncle's home, a beautiful property right on the ocean. It was magical, nothing short of amazing. The air was thick with the aroma of goat soup, curried dishes, and the sweet, intoxicating scent of rum punch. Music pulsed through the warm evening, and people danced with a joy that was infectious. The whole community came out to celebrate with us. I felt, for the first time in a very long time, like a princess.

Amidst all the revelry, the MC's words during his opening speech struck a chord within me, words that would, in time, feel chillingly prophetic. After the initial greetings, he looked out at us, at the assembled guests, and said, "In any relationship, communication is the key. If there is no communication, it means vital things aren't being shared, and that is where problems begin. If you don't communicate, it's going to be a problem." At the time, I nodded along, thinking it was sound advice. Only later, much later, would I realize how those words were a direct forecast of the profound silence and unspoken grievances that would eventually shake the very foundations of our marriage.

After the reception, many guests were unable to make the long journey back to their homes in the "bush," as the rural areas were called. The house was filled with sleeping bodies. People slept wherever they could—on sofas, on chairs, on the floor. My new husband and I ended up sharing a bed with several relatives, sleeping crosswise just to fit. It was not the romantic first night I had imagined, but it was real, raw, and communal.

The following week was a precious interlude, a time spent visiting family and friends, basking in the warm glow of newlywed life. But the shadow of my approaching departure back to the States loomed heavy. All too soon, the day came for me to return to America. The goodbye at the airport was excruciating. Tears streamed down my face, and I saw the unmistakable glisten in Howard's eyes as well. This tall, strong policeman, usually so composed, was visibly shaken.

The flight back home felt like an eternity. The moment I walked through my front door in New Jersey, I rushed to the phone, my fingers fumbling with the dial. When he answered, his voice was thick with emotion. He confessed he was still at the airport, huddled in a corner, unable to bring himself to leave the place where we had last been together. He couldn't believe I was truly gone. Our connection, so vibrant and alive when we were together, now had to stretch across the ocean once more, sustained by tearful phone calls and the fervent hope of reunion.

It took about a year or two, filled with endless paperwork and anxious waiting, but Howard was eventually granted a visitor's visa. He came to America. After a couple of visits back and forth, he stayed. Our married life, truly together under one roof, finally began in the United States. In those early days, there was a sweetness, a sense of shared purpose. He was, in many ways, a wonderful partner. He cleaned the house meticulously, cooked delicious meals, and washed our clothes. We worked well as a team. When I was deep in the throes of nursing school, he was my rock. He had this incredible personality, a sense of humor that could light up any room and make me laugh until my sides ached. It felt like we were building something solid, something real.

But slowly, insidiously, the dark side I hadn't fully acknowledged began to emerge. The women. It wasn't just a casual flirtation here or there; it was a consistent, heartbreaking pattern. It started with a letter. I found it tucked away in his bag, a single piece of paper that would unravel the life I thought we were building. It was from a young woman named Kareen, someone he'd met at the HVAC school he was attending in New Jersey. The letter was a torrent of emotion; she was madly in love with him, desperately pleading with him to leave me. She'd even pointed out, quite cruelly, that I was twelve years his senior and, in her eyes, not good enough for him.

The words hit me like a physical blow. The air left my lungs. I confronted him, the letter shaking in my hand, my voice trembling with a mixture of rage and disbelief. That night, he came home blind drunk, vomiting, a pathetic mess of apologies and tearful promises that it would never, ever happen again. And in my desperate need to believe, in my hunger for the stability I thought we were building, I chose to forgive him.

Life settled into a precarious rhythm. Howard was, for the most part, a very good stepfather to my children. My eldest daughter, Sydonie, had by then joined us in the US from Jamaica. My second daughter, the one whose early life had been marked by so much hardship and separation, remained in Jamaica, a constant, quiet ache in my heart that never truly went away. Seven long years into our marriage, after the emotional and physical rollercoaster of reversing my tubal ligation and undergoing IVF—a process during which Howard was surprisingly supportive, giving me the injections himself—I gave birth to our daughter, Erin, in November 1995. A wave of profound joy and renewed hope washed over me. Surely, I thought, this precious new life, a child born of our shared desire, would solidify our bond. This would be a new beginning.

But the infidelity, like a stubborn weed, persisted, choking the life from our marriage no matter how many times I tried to pull it out.

Then, in a turn of events that defied all medical explanation, another miracle occurred. Despite my tubes supposedly having been tied again after Erin's birth, I found myself inexplicably pregnant. My doctors were shocked. Our son, Najee, was born via C-section, arriving on Howard's own birthday. The delivering doctor, upon examining me post-surgery, was in disbelief. "Her tubes are still intact!" he exclaimed to the nurses in the operating room. "This is a miracle child!" And he truly was. A testament, perhaps, to a plan far greater than my own understanding.

Yet, even these profound blessings, these miracle children, could not ultimately heal the deep-rooted issues in our marriage. Howard, the man who could be so charming, so supportive, so loving, never truly stopped his affairs. His mouth remained sealed, a fortress of unspoken truths and unaddressed problems, and the silence between us grew into a chasm. The MC's words from our wedding day echoed in my mind, a constant, haunting refrain: "If there is no communication... it's going to be a problem." And a problem it had become, an insurmountable one.

The constant betrayal, the humiliation, the breaking up of the family I had so desperately tried to build, began to take a toll not just on my heart, but on my mind. I was still working a full-time job, still pastoring a growing church, still counseling people through their own issues, all while my own world was crumbling. The smiling mask I wore grew heavier each day.

People underestimate the reality of spiritual warfare, the insidious way it attacks the mind. It's not always a loud, dramatic battle; sometimes it's a quiet, creeping darkness. There were moments when I felt something had a hold of me, tying up my tongue, making it impossible to even muster the strength to pray. I'd be in bed, wanting to cry out to God, but feeling a suffocating bondage, a weight so heavy I didn't even want to see the light of day. It would come over me in the snap of a finger, a rushing wind of despair.

I remember one night, trying to find a moment of escape at the movies. As I sat there in the dark, a horrifying sensation washed over me. It felt as if my body was still sitting in the theater seat, but my mind, my spirit, my very consciousness, was detaching, floating away. It was a terrifying out-of-body experience. I wanted to get up, to run outside and somehow catch my mind before it left me completely, but I was paralyzed. I couldn't explain it. If I told someone, they would think I was insane. In that moment of sheer panic, I had to make a choice. I had to get a hold of myself, to purpose in my mind that I would not fall apart, that I would trust God even when I felt like I was losing my mind.

The attacks grew more intense. One afternoon, I was in my kitchen, and suddenly, that same wave of inexplicable terror washed over me. I felt a desperate, primal urge to flee. I ran out of my house, barefoot, keys in hand, and jumped into my car. I drove frantically up the street, pulled over, and begged a strange man on the sidewalk to take me to the hospital. He refused, likely thinking I was deranged. Somehow, I managed to drive myself to the emergency room. I don't remember how I got there. All I remember is running into the hospital, barefoot and terrified, feeling as if the rest of my sanity had just come crashing down.

Spiritual warfare is real. For those who have never encountered it, it's easy to dismiss. But I lived it. It wasn't just in my head; it manifested in my home. We had built a brand-new house, solid and secure. Yet, during this period, wall paintings would inexplicably fly off the walls and smash on the floor. I remember one incident so clearly: the sickening crash, the shattered glass, and then the chilling discovery. The nail was still firmly in the wall, and the cord on the back of the frame was still intact. It was as if an invisible hand had lifted it off the wall and hurled it to the ground. These were not just marital problems; this was a severe, supernatural attack.

In a last-ditch effort to salvage what was left, or perhaps to simply escape the oppressive spiritual atmosphere, it was during this tumultuous period that I truly surrendered my life to Christ and was saved while in New Jersey. This became my anchor. I immersed myself in Bible school and threw every ounce of my being into ministry. Later when I relocated to PA, Soul Winners Pentecostal Church was born, my pain becoming my purpose.

But the marriage could not be saved. After nearly thirty years—a lifetime—I found the strength to file for divorce. The pain was undeniable, a deep ache, especially for our daughter, Erin, who had been incredibly close to her father and had witnessed far too much. Yet, through it all, sustained by the unwavering grace of God and the support of a few faithful believers, I found the strength to rebuild. I grieved for what was, for what could have been, but I also thanked God. That marriage, with all its pain, had shaped me, strengthened me, and ultimately prepared me for the ministry He had called me to. He gave me beauty for my ashes. Every tear, every betrayal, every moment of despair, I now see, was not random. It was a necessary, painful part of a divine preparation.

To the women reading this who feel stuck, who question their worth, who wonder if love will ever come easy, I see you. I was you. And I want you to know: You are not your pain. You are not your past. You are worthy of a love that doesn't hurt, a life that doesn't drain you, and a God who will never, ever leave you. Hold on. For with Christ in the vessel, you can, and you will, smile at the storm.

SELF-REFLECTION QUESTIONS:

What signs helped you distinguish hope from haste in a fast-moving relationship?

How do you honor your intuition when excitement (family, travel, wedding plans) is loud and fear is quiet?

Which non-negotiables about communication would you put in place before saying "I do"?

How do culture, community, or family expectations shape your view of marriage—and where do your own values differ?

If you were to write your vows today, what promises would protect both your heart and your future self?

Chapter 16

From Mess to Ministry

"I wasn't just called—I was crushed first."

Before the ministry, before the pulpit, before the healing—I was a mess. A quiet, soul-crushing kind of mess. The kind that builds slowly and silently while you're still showing up for everyone else. Smiling. Serving. Functioning. Until one day, you're standing in front of a mirror asking yourself, "How did I get here?"

My home was full of people, yet I felt alone. I was married, yet emotionally abandoned. I was doing ministry work, yet still bleeding from wounds I hadn't fully acknowledged or healed. I was tired. I was grieving. I was pouring from an empty cup. And still, I was trying to be everything for everyone.

That's the part people don't see. The version of you that gets dressed for church after crying all night. The woman who lays hands on others but can barely lift her own. The wife who is hosting Bible study while her marriage is falling apart in silence.

That was me.

I didn't step into ministry from a place of spiritual superiority. I stepped in dragging the baggage of betrayal, insecurity, and survival. My calling didn't come with a spotlight. It came with silence. It came when I had nothing else to give and everything to heal. There's a misconception that ministry starts at the microphone, but mine started on the bathroom floor.

When I say "mess," I mean it. Emotionally. Mentally. Spiritually. I was still wrestling with rejection, still crying over childhood trauma, still trying to piece together a sense of self-worth from broken relationships and broken promises. I was trying to outrun the labels the world had put on me and the ones I had put on myself. Yet somehow, God kept whispering to me, "Daughter, you're still the one I want."

At first, I ran from the call. I didn't feel qualified. I didn't have the right credentials. I didn't have a perfect marriage. I didn't come from a long line of pastors. I was a woman who had been through hell and still carried the residue most days. I wasn't polished or put together. I was rough around the edges and easily triggered because I didn't know my identity in Christ. But maybe that's why God called me and figured He can still use ALL my mess.

I started ministering before I even knew it was ministry. Cooking meals and handing them out to the hungry. Listening to broken women pour out their stories. Praying for people while I was still battling my own spiritual storms. There was no church building as yet and no sign outside. Just a burning compassion inside me that wouldn't let me rest. I just couldn't shake this desire off.

Because I knew what it meant to feel forgotten. I knew what it meant to cry myself to sleep. I knew what it felt like to be spiritually starving. And I couldn't sit still while others were drowning in the same kind of pain.

Ministry found me when I wasn't looking. It met me in hospital waiting rooms and on shelter floors. It spoke through me when I didn't even know what to say. And little by little, I stopped hiding behind the image of who I thought I was supposed to be. I let God use the real me—the flawed, imperfect, healing me.

The true genesis of my ministry can be traced back to the birth of my last son, Najee. He's 27 now, a grown man, but when he was just a baby, I took him to church for his christening, his dedication to the Lord. It was during that service, as the pastor made the altar call, that something shifted irrevocably within me. I found myself walking towards that altar, weary from a lifetime of mess that I was ready to surrender to God.

After I left the altar that day, a young lady, a minister from the church's ministry team, approached me. She began to call, to minister, to gently guide me. I must confess, I resisted at first. My heart was guarded, my trust in people, in institutions, in the church was fractured. But she persisted with pure kindness. And as I finally allowed myself to get involved, as we began to venture out into the streets for ministry and outreach, a realization dawned on me. This was it. This was for me.

As I met people on the streets, listened to their stories, saw their raw hunger, their homelessness, their brokenness, I saw myself. Their struggles mirrored my own. The vacant stares of those without a roof over their heads, the quiet desperation in the eyes of those who felt alone, was a language my heart understood. This wasn't just a ministry for me. It was bigger than me. That day, something ignited within me, a fire of compassion and purpose, and I took off running, and I haven't stopped since.

God started to orchestrate encounters that deepened my conviction to serve Him and to start a ministry. I vividly remember a young man named Godfrey, who is no longer with us. May God rest his soul. We met him on the street one evening; I think he was on his way home from work. We ministered to him, invited him to church. He came, accepted Christ, and was baptized. He lived with his sister, but shortly after dedicating his life to Christ, numerous challenges arose. His sister, not sharing his newfound faith, began threatening to throw him out.

One night, my phone rang. It was Godfrey, his voice strained. "Pastor," he said, "I have nowhere to go. My sister put me out."

Without a second thought, I drove to where he was, picked him up, and brought him into my home. I gave him a room in our basement. It was in that moment, seeing his vulnerability, his immediate and desperate need, that the urgency of outreach ministry became clear for me. There were so many Godfreys out there, so many souls teetering on the edge, needing not just a prayer, but a helping hand.

Godfrey eventually found his own place, but life, as it often does, threw him another curveball. He lost his apartment and ended up back with his sister. I was a practicing nurse by then. One evening, he called, complaining of not feeling well. He'd been to the emergency room, he said, but they'd treated him and sent him home. Two days later, I was at the hairdresser when my phone rang with an urgent summons from my girlfriend: "Come to the emergency room, now! It's Godfrey."

My heart sank. When I arrived, I learned the devastating news. Godfrey, only in his 30s, had suffered a massive heart attack. They were performing emergency open-heart surgery. To see this young man, who had so recently found faith, now fighting for his life, without a stable home, without resources—it tore at me. My passion, my calling to serve those in crisis, grew even stronger. From that point on, there was no turning back.

My past experiences—the ache of homelessness, the repeated sting of heartbreaks, the silent terror of abuse—weren't just scars; they became the foundation of my ministry. To be homeless, to not have a space to call your own, a place where you feel safe and anchored, is a disorienting and heartbreaking experience. I remember the sting of not having my own stove to cook a warm meal. Everyone who truly knows me knows I love to eat and I find comfort in the simple act of preparing food. I remember the humiliation of not having a private bathroom for a simple shower.

During one of my darkest periods in New York, I was homeless. Each night, I'd scrape together $25 to rent a dingy hotel room, just for a few hours of troubled sleep. And then, come morning, I'd be back out on the streets, walking, just walking, trying to fill the empty hours until it was time to go to my low-paying job. Then, after work, back to the hotel, another $25, another restless night, followed by another day of aimless wandering. This cycle of instability, of never feeling secure, went on for what felt like an eternity. So, when I encountered someone like Godfrey, without a home, the memory of my own desolation would come rushing back to me. I could identify with his fear, his uncertainty, because I had lived it. It wasn't just sympathy I felt; it was a deep, resonant empathy.

And then there were the countless faces I encountered while working in the substance abuse clinic for the City of East Orange—though the details must remain confidential. I saw so much suffering: women, often with young children in tow, with nowhere to go. I visited homes where the conditions were so heartbreaking that it brought me right back to the rawest moments of my own past, the times when I had nothing, no place to lay my head, no family to turn to.

And perhaps one of the most severe memories of all: being homeless and pregnant with my second daughter in Jamaica. Fleeing abuse, hoping for refuge with family who couldn't, or wouldn't, take me in. Hiding my pregnancy by "banging my belly," tying it down tightly with cloth, a desperate attempt to conceal my vulnerability. Giving birth which started in a pit latrine, with no prenatal care, no diapers, no clean clothes for my newborn, feeling, in that moment, no different from an animal birthing its young in the wild, unprepared and alone to the bed.

These experiences carved into my soul an unshakeable compassion, an almost desperate hunger to alleviate the suffering of others. It's why, even now, in my current home, I've opened my doors to those in need. Just last year, I had two people living with me who were homeless. One has since moved on, but the other is still here. It's a pattern in my life, a calling I can't ignore. When someone tells me they have no place to live, it's like a switch flips inside me. I remember where I came from, and I simply cannot turn away. My former church secretary lived in my home for eight years. Yes, sometimes people take advantage, sometimes you get hurt, but the pull to help, to provide sanctuary, is way too strong.

It's this deep-seated drive that has led me to envision the next phase of my ministry. Right here, in the building that houses Soul Winners Pentecostal Church—a building I own, a testament to God's faithfulness—there's unused office space. People have pointed out its potential. "You could create apartments here," they've said, "temporary housing for the homeless." And that's precisely what I'm looking into now. Last week, someone told me about three women with babies, out in the rain, with nowhere to go. The need is so great. I'm currently exploring grants, trying to refinance the church mortgage, to find a way to transform this empty space into a haven, a place of temporary refuge. That's where my heart is, that's where my ministry is constantly leading me.

I know there are organizations out there, like Community Action with their Sixth Street Shelter, doing incredible work. The funding exists. It's just a matter of navigating the system, of meeting the right people, of cracking open that door of opportunity. I believe God has placed people in my life, like Jacinth, to help bring these visions to fruition.

When people ask me what "true, genuine ministry" means, it's a question that cuts to the core of my being. I wasn't raised in the church. My early encounters with organized religion in Jamaica were fleeting and superficial, meaning little to a young woman preoccupied with survival. When you're homeless, when you're unstable, sermons and hymns often go in one ear and out the other. It was only after Najee's birth, after I truly surrendered my life at that altar, that I began to understand.

My initial perception of "church" was one of holiness, of kind and respectful people, a place of ultimate security. But as I delved deeper, as I studied the Word and observed the landscape of modern Christianity, I saw a different picture, one that often broke my heart. I saw deception, pride, people using the name of Jesus Christ as a front for their own agendas, sometimes even for evil. Initially, this filled me with anger. But God, in His wisdom, allowed me to stay, to see, to understand. He didn't call me to start a church; it just happened, organically, out of the outreach work I was already doing—feeding the homeless, visiting prisoners, singing in nursing homes, bringing Christmas gifts to hospital patients.

The battles I've faced in this ministry haven't come from the unsaved world. They've come from within the church itself, often from men of God who couldn't accept a woman in leadership. My calling is different from the commercialized, fame-driven gospel that seems so prevalent today. My hunger, my thirst, is for people to encounter the undiluted truth of Jesus Christ. Not to be coerced, not to be manipulated, not to have the gospel used as a bait-and-switch tactic, 50% truth and 50% lies. The Word of God, in its pure, unadulterated form, is enough to win souls, to convict hearts, to transform lives. We don't need to add to it or twist it.

What also troubles me deeply is the denominationalism, the divisions. One God, one Body of Christ, yet we segregate ourselves into so many different houses—Pentecostal, Baptist, Catholic, Muslim—often refusing to fellowship with one another. If we can't find unity here on earth, how can we expect to share one heaven? The Bible says that one of the things God hates most is he who sows discord among brethren. When the church itself is divided, when pastors of different denominations refuse to fellowship, what message are we sending to the world watching? We, the church, are meant to be the head, the leaders, preaching peace, love, unity, understanding. If the head of the stream is polluted, that pollution will inevitably flow down to the pews, into our communities, and across nations.

I see so many social media-driven ministries today, leaders focused more on gaining followers than on truly gaining souls for Christ. It's become about numbers, about platforms, about personal brand. That's not the gospel I know. I was a club girl, loved to dance, and loved to party. My attire was often provocative, practically naked by some standards. That was who I was. If I, in that state, had walked into a church and been judged for my short shorts or my exposed panty line, I would have turned right back around. The Bible says, "Come as you are." It's not the pastor, not the usher, not the fellow congregant who changes us. It is the Holy Spirit, working through love and prayer, who strips away the old and makes us new. When people try to do the stripping, it's temporary, often judgmental. When the Holy Spirit transforms, it's for good, it's forever. That's the true gospel and true transformation.

The turning point for me, the moment I knew I needed to go deeper, to equip myself further, was born out of this hunger for more of God, for a more profound understanding. When I first got saved, the music drew me in, the vibrant, joyful sounds that resonated with my love for dance. But as I attended Bible studies, as the Word was broken down, something began to tug at my heart. I became intensely hungry for spiritual truth. I started fasting with the women's ministry, and during those times of dedicated prayer, I began to have extraordinary experiences.

I remember praying desperately for a bigger vehicle to transport people to church. My little Honda Accord was leased, a financial arrangement I barely understood at the time. I walked into a car dealership, told them my need, and through a series of what can only be described as divinely orchestrated "mistakes" on their part, I drove out with a seven-seater Honda Odyssey. They'd overlooked the lease, undervalued my trade-in. When they called me back, expecting me to return the van, the manager, baffled by their own errors, simply said, "We made a mistake. Just pay an extra $50 a month, and the car is yours." I knew then, with absolute certainty, that God had blinded their eyes so I could have that vehicle to do His work.

Another time, I needed money for a dinner event and had nothing but $15 to my name. It was a Sunday, no mail, no obvious way for funds to appear. I prayed, "God, I need your provision, I need money." Later that day, my doorbell rang. It was a man who, six months prior, had asked to rent garage space behind my house. He'd come to give me the down payment. I jumped for joy. It had to be God.

I began to see lights, to have visions during worship. Everything I prayed for, God seemed to provide. These supernatural encounters, these undeniable proofs of God's presence and power in my life, fueled my desire to go to seminary, to truly understand the scriptures, to be equipped not just with passion, but with sound doctrine.

When I enrolled in seminary, I was terrified. I was older than most of the other students. I hadn't been in school in years. But I knew that if I was going to lead others, I needed to be fed too. Seminary wasn't about earning a title; it was about finally understanding the depth of the call that had chased me down.

The deeper I went in my studies, the more God revealed my identity to me. Not as a victim of my past, but as a vessel for His glory. I started to release the shame I had carried for so long. The shame of failed relationships. The shame of not having a picture-perfect family. The shame of decisions I'd made while trying to survive. I began to see that none of it disqualified me—it equipped me.

I wasn't called because I was perfect. I was called because I knew pain. And that pain gave me compassion. It gave me language for the silent struggles of others. It gave me authority to speak to things that textbooks don't teach. Because healing doesn't always come in scripture alone—it often comes in knowing that someone else has walked through the fire and lived to tell the story.

My journey as a woman in ministry has been one with giants, and those giants have almost always been men. They quote Paul—"a woman should be silent in church"—and question my right to lead. They wonder how I, with no formal religious upbringing, no seminary degree at the time, could have built this ministry, this church building. The truth is, I didn't plan any of it. I never aspired to be a pastor, never dreamed of having a church.

I didn't know how to preach. It all just happened. It was God. And as the Bible says, God often takes the "base things of this world to confound the wise." He doesn't call the qualified; He qualifies the called. That scripture is etched on my heart.

I had no advantageous beginning, no Christian heritage to lean on. This ministry started in my garage, with just me and my two sisters, praying, just praying. It grew from a gospel concert I organized, one of the coldest nights of the year, where over 300 people showed up, to the astonishment of many. The jealousy and sabotage I've faced, often from other ministries, has been heartbreaking. I've watched men I trusted try to undermine what God was building. In 2015, our boiler broke, pipes burst, and we were displaced. I thought it was the end. Lawsuits followed. But God sustained us. In 2021, we had a split, nearly 90% of the congregation left. Again, I thought, "This is it." But God ministered to our hearts. And through it all, the mortgage has always been paid, the lights have stayed on, the water has kept running. It's been nothing but the grace of God.

I've learned to put on my fighting shoes and my boxing gloves, spiritually speaking. And that's why I'm still standing.

It's been twenty long, hard, but ultimately glorious years. Many women in scripture—Eve, Mary, Esther—were used mightily by God, often in defiance of cultural norms. Their stories give me courage. I never truly "backslid" in the traditional sense once I committed my life to Christ in Jersey. My ministry didn't start within the four walls of a church building, with a pulpit and a microphone. It started on the streets, in the homeless shelters, in the prisons, in the nursing homes. That's where the true church often is. And that's where my heart will always be.

So many churches have been birthed out of this one, people who caught the vision and went on to do their own work. But the core of it, for me, has always been about seeing the person, not their circumstance, not their sin, but their soul, hungry for the love and truth of Jesus. I attract those who are broken, those who have stories like mine, because they are a mirror, reflecting the journey God has brought me through.

The scriptures that keep me grounded are Philippians 4:13: "I can do all things through Christ who strengthens me." And Psalm 34:1: "I will bless the Lord at all times; His praise shall continually be in my mouth." When the storms rage, and they do, especially the higher you climb in ministry, I remember Daniel in the lion's den, Esther risking her life for her people. I tell God, "If You did it for them, You can do it for me." I ask Him to examine my heart, to reveal anything not of Him. And I surround myself with a small, trusted circle of prayer warriors, women of faith who lift me up when I'm faltering.

Faith isn't easy. Trusting a God you cannot see, relying on Him to fix what seems irrevocably broken—it takes an unwavering, deeply personal commitment. It's not about religious performance; it's about a genuine, transformative encounter with the living God. And I pray that everyone, no matter their background, their beliefs, their brokenness, would dare to give Jesus a try. Just try. Because when His truth truly takes root in your heart, you will never be the same.

If I were to leave a legacy, if people who never met me were to read my story or encounter my ministry, I would want them to take away one crucial thing: humility. God resists the proud but gives grace to the humble. Humility is the key. It means waiting on the Lord, even when every fiber of your being wants to fight, to control, to fix it yourself. It means taking the lower seat and allowing God to exalt you in His time.

The ultimate impact I want my ministry to leave behind is one of authentic transformation. I would turn over in my grave if this ministry fell into the hands of someone who squandered resources, who lorded their position over God's people, who abused the vulnerable, especially children. My deepest desire is for this place, this work, to be a beacon of genuine love, unwavering truth, and profound healing, a testament to the God who took my mess and, against all odds, turned it into a ministry.

That's when I realized: ministry wasn't about being above the mess. It was about being honest in the middle of it. I watched God take every broken piece of my life and turn it into a stepping stone for someone else. I became a midwife for other women's breakthroughs. Not because I had all the answers, but because I had survived. Because I knew what it meant to feel unworthy and still show up.

Ministry, for me, is not a performance. It's a posture. A daily yes. A willingness to be vulnerable, even when it hurts. And my God, it hurts. But it was worth it.

To the woman reading this who feels like her life is too messy to be used, let me tell you: God does His best work in the mess. You don't need to be perfect. You just need to be honest. Your tears are ministry. Your survival is a sermon. Your healing journey is a revival in the making.

If God could use me—a single mother, a former club dancer, a woman who once chased love and lost herself in the process—then surely, He can use you. You are not disqualified by what you've been through. You are qualified because you came through it.

And what felt like the end of you? Was just the beginning of ministry.

SELF-REFLECTION QUESTIONS:

Where has your deepest pain hinted at a purpose you've been avoiding or afraid to name?

Whose struggle do you recognize as a mirror of your own—and what simple act of service can you offer this week?

How do you tell the difference between performing faith and practicing it with honesty and love?

What grudges or church hurts still harden your heart—and what would forgiveness look like today?

If you trusted God's timing, not your timeline, what next faithful step would you take right now?

Chapter 17

A Love That Heals—"The Total Package"

Romans 10:9–10 (KJV)

9 That if thou shalt confess with thy mouth the Lord Jesus, and shalt believe in thine heart that God hath raised him from the dead, thou shalt be saved.

10 For with the heart man believeth unto righteousness; and with the mouth confession is made unto salvation.

After a lifetime of surviving heartbreak, betrayal, and the kind of trauma that leaves invisible bruises on the soul, I reached a point of stillness. Not defeat, but surrender. A sacred kind of release. I had given God everything: my past, my pain, my praise, my uncertainty, and even my dreams of partnership. Romance? Love? I had closed that door and bolted it shut. My only focus was surviving the storm I was in, continuing the ministry that had become my lifeline. I had no desire to complicate things with another relationship. Honestly, I didn't think I had space in my heart for one.

I wasn't alone, though. I had my small circle of sisters—great women of God, friends who held me up in prayer and wisdom, who stood with me when I couldn't stand on my own—and my family. I was content in that season. I truly believed that was enough.

Then came a Sunday morning that changed everything. I was at the church, Soul Winners Pentecostal, bustling about, attending to the usual pre-service preparations. It was around 10:30 a.m., and our service was scheduled to commence at 11:00. One of the deacons approached me, with a sense of urgency in his demeanor. "Pastor," he said, "there's a gentleman outside who needs to speak with you. He says someone needs prayer."

My initial thought was practical. *It's nearly service time. There's no distance in prayer; we can pray for them during the service.* But then a gentle nudge, that still, small voice I'd learned to heed, prompted me to ask, "Where are they?"

"In the overflow room, Pastor," the deacon replied.

"Alright," I said, a sense of duty overriding my pre-service routine. "Let me go and speak with them."

I quickly instructed another minister on what needed to be done to start the service, and then, with the deacon by my side, I headed towards the overflow room. As I entered, I saw a gentleman and a lady walking towards the sanctuary. They looked distressed. The deacon had already conveyed their need.

I approached the gentleman directly. "I understand someone is in need of prayer?"

"Yes, Pastor," he replied, his voice heavy with concern. "It's my wife. She's in the hospital. She needs prayer."

My mind immediately went to healing prayer, the kind so often requested in such circumstances. "Is she a Christian?" I asked gently.

"No, Pastor, she's not."

A sense of urgency, different now, more profound, settled over me. This wasn't just about physical healing; this was about something eternal. I turned to the minister I'd left in charge. "Please, carry on with the service. I need to go to the hospital."

Without hesitation, accompanied by the deacon, I left the church and headed to St. Luke's Anderson Hospital. When we arrived, we made our way upstairs to the indicated room. Lying in the hospital bed was a woman who looked frail, almost translucent. I knew nothing about her, except that she was not a Christian, and her husband had sought prayer. I walked to the foot of her bed, a silent prayer forming in my heart, and then, instinctively, I reached out and gently took hold of her two feet. I began to pray, a simple, earnest plea for her soul. Then, I moved to the side of her bed and continued to pray.

After a few moments, I asked about her condition. I learned she had cancer, a particularly aggressive form, and was in its final stages. The air in the room was thick with unspoken grief. I leaned closer to her and asked softly, "Are you a Christian?"

Her voice was barely a whisper, a pale thread of sound. "No."

"Would you like to be?"

A flicker of something in her eyes, a faint nod. "Yes."

"Okay," I said, my voice gentle, trying to convey the immense love and urgency I felt. "I'm going to ask you a couple of questions. Just respond as you feel led."

She whispered, her breath shallow, "Take your time with me. I'm very weak. I can't talk loud."

"Don't worry," I reassured her. "I'm going to read a scripture to you. You don't have to say anything aloud unless you want to. Just a yes or no in your heart will do."

I opened my Bible to Romans, chapter 10, verses 9 and 10:

"That if thou shalt confess with thy mouth the Lord Jesus, and shalt believe in thine heart that God hath raised him from the dead, thou shalt be saved. For with the heart man believeth unto righteousness; and with the mouth confession is made unto salvation."

I read the words slowly, clearly, letting their profound truth fill the space between us. "Is this your belief?" I asked her.

A faint, yet definite, "Yes."

"Do you believe that God raised Jesus from the dead?"

"Yes."

"And is this what you are confessing in your heart right now?"

"Yes."

A wave of peace washed over me. "Then," I said, my voice filled with a quiet joy, "you are saved."

I prayed with her again, a prayer of thanksgiving, of welcoming her into the family of God. Shortly after, I left the hospital and returned to the church. I arrived in the height of the service, my heart overflowing. I took the microphone and began to testify, to share with the congregation the beautiful, sacred encounter that had just taken place. I was so excited, so moved by the power of God's grace. It was only at the end of the service that I saw him, the husband, and his sister. I hadn't realized they had followed me back from the hospital and had been present throughout the entire service. I greeted them briefly, still reeling from the experience, and then they departed.

That was Sunday morning. On Wednesday, I was at work when I suddenly remembered the woman in the hospital. I felt compelled to call the husband, whose name I now knew was Hugh, to inquire about his wife.

"Pastor" he said when he answered, his voice somber. "I'm so sorry... she passed away."

My heart constricted. "Oh, Hugh, I am so, so sorry to hear that."

"Yes," he continued, a tremor in his voice. "She passed away Monday morning, around 6:00 a.m."

The timing stunned me. I had been with her around 10:45 a.m. on Sunday morning. She had accepted Jesus Christ into her heart just hours, mere hours, before she drew her last breath. "Wow," I breathed, the significance of it all settling upon me.

Then, Hugh said something that took me completely by surprise. "Pastor, I was so glad you came. And... I would be honored if you would do the funeral."

A funeral. For a woman I had met only once, for a family I barely knew. Yet, the request felt right, a divine appointment. He explained that his wife, in those final moments before I arrived, had woken from a semi-coma. Other pastors had visited, but she hadn't responded. That Sunday morning, however, she had stirred, her eyes fluttering open, and had spoken with an unexpected clarity and urgency.

"Find me a pastor," she had told Hugh. "Find me one now!" She had insisted it was important, that they *had* to come. Her daughter, also a nurse, later told me that if she hadn't known her mother better, she would have thought she was hallucinating from medication. But it was real. Her mother had then begun pointing around the room, her voice filled with awe, "I see Jesus! Jesus is in my room! There He is! Go get me a pastor, now!"

And so, Hugh had left her bedside and had gone searching, a desperate husband on a holy mission, and he had found me. What he didn't tell me until later was that they had recorded everything that happened in that hospital room on Sunday morning—my arrival, my ministering to his wife, her acceptance of Christ. It was all captured, a poignant testament to her final, faith-filled moments.

The funeral was held the following Saturday. When I arrived, I was astonished by the sheer number of people present. It seemed the story of the pastor who had left her own church service to minister to a dying woman had spread. I learned that before coming to Soul Winners, Hugh had first gone to Greater Shiloh. They had apparently told him it was too close to their service time and they couldn't help. He then went to another church in Easton, but its doors were closed. It was as he was driving past our church, on his way home, dejected, that he'd said to his sister, "Here's another church. Even if it's a priest in there, I'm going to get them to come to the hospital." That's how God works—in the most unexpected, divinely orchestrated ways.

I delivered the eulogy and ministered to the grieving family. The woman's son and his girlfriend accepted Christ during the service. Afterwards, Hugh and his son began attending Soul Winners regularly. They never missed a service.

About three Sundays later, we were in the sanctuary after service, discussing funeral arrangements for a church member whose father had passed away in Jamaica. Hugh, who had been walking past, overheard our conversation and stopped. "Pastor," he said, "I'd like to go to the funeral with you. I'm so grateful for what you did for my wife and my family, I'd like to return the favor."

We were all thrilled. Hugh, we learned, was a pilot (though not actively flying at the time), and immediately, there was excited chatter about free tickets. He then said to me directly, "If you're going, Pastor, I'd be happy to be your chauffeur while you're there. Kingston can be rough." I readily accepted his kind offer.

I flew to Jamaica on a Wednesday, checking into the Grand Bahia Principe in Runaway Bay with my daughter, Erin. Hugh arrived on Thursday. He called to let me know he was at his hotel and would see me the next morning. True to his word, he picked us up on Friday. He was the perfect gentleman, chauffeuring us to visit my brothers, taking Erin and me to get our hair and nails done, and for a bit of shopping. It was a delightful day. He dropped us back at our hotel, promising to pick us up Saturday morning for the funeral in Kingston.

At the funeral, after I took my seat, I expected Hugh to sit beside my daughter. Instead, he made his way around and sat directly next to me. A little flutter went through me. *Does he like me?* I wondered, then quickly dismissed it. *Maybe he just doesn't want to sit next to Erin and have people talk, men liking younger girls and all that.*

Towards the end of the service, Erin went to buy some peanut brittle, a Jamaican treat I love. As the service concluded and the crowd began to file out, I was looking for Erin, anticipating my candy. Suddenly, I felt a distinct touch on my back. A sensation, electric and warm, shot through my entire body, a feeling unlike anything I had ever experienced before or since. I spun around, searching for the source, but no one was close enough to have touched me. A shiver went down my spine. *Was it a ghost?* The thought, absurd as it was, actually crossed my mind. The feeling, that inexplicable touch, lingered with me, unsettling and intriguing, as we made our way to the car.

I wanted to ask Hugh if it had been him, but I was too embarrassed, too flustered by the strange chemistry that was undeniably sparking between us. We drove to KFC for a quick bite. I was quiet, lost in thought, replaying that moment, that touch. Later, we went to the repast. It was late when it ended, and Hugh kindly offered us rooms at his house nearby, as it was too far to travel back to St. Ann that night. I shared a room with my pastor friend. I was exhausted and fell asleep almost instantly.

The next morning, I went to check on Erin. As I entered her room, I saw her on her hands and knees, searching the floor.

"Erin, what are you looking for?" I asked.

"Mommy, I lost my eyelashes!" she exclaimed.

A wave of déjà vu, or perhaps something more, washed over me. I ran back to my friend. "Oh my gosh, you won't believe this! Erin is in there looking for her eyelashes!"

My friend was stunned. "How did you know?" she asked. I couldn't explain it; the thought had just come to me.

Hugh had gone out to buy breakfast. We ate, dropped my friend off, and then he drove Erin and me back to St. Ann. He was due to fly back to America the next day. At my hotel, as we said goodbye, Erin hugged him and thanked him. I hugged him too, and then, on impulse, I squeezed his hand. The moment I did it, a jolt went through me. I practically fled into my hotel room, not daring to look back, my cheeks burning. *What had I just done?* I, a pastor, was feeling things, experiencing a connection that was both thrilling and terrifying.

An hour later, I called to see if he'd made it back to Kingston safely. No answer. I tried again. Still nothing. The next morning, Monday, he called. "I missed my flight," he said, with such disappointment. As a pilot, he often flew standby, and he'd been bumped. We spoke briefly, no mention of the hand squeeze, and then he was gone.

Tuesday morning, back in my hotel room in Jamaica, after Erin had gone down for breakfast, I felt it again—that sensation, like someone had punched me in the back, pushing me forward. I began to panic. My heart, already prone to irregularities, started to race. My heart rate soared to 140, my blood pressure to a frightening 190/100. I called the front desk; a nurse rushed up. I ended up in the emergency room at St. Ann's Bay Hospital. Thankfully, my sister worked there as a nurse. By the time they checked me out, everything had returned to normal.

That same day, I texted Hugh, who was now back in America, and told him what had happened. He was full of concern. "I'm so sorry I left," he said over the phone. "If I had been there, I would have taken care of you."

The following day, I flew back to America. The strange cardiac episodes continued. One night, I woke up, my heart pounding violently—141, 142 beats per minute, blood pressure through the roof. Another trip to the emergency room, more tests, but still no definitive answers.

Throughout this frightening period, Hugh was a constant presence, albeit over the phone. We talked every day. I shared my health scares; he spoke of his late wife, of his grief, of his children. We started going out for dinner on weekends, meeting to talk, to share, to simply be in each other's company. And slowly, gently, a deep and abiding bond began to form.

I met his son, Hugh Jr.—"UJ"—a wonderful young man who instantly captured a piece of my heart. Hugh had three biological children and four stepchildren from his late wife's previous marriage. His life, in many ways, mirrored my own—the complexities of blended families and past relationships. He even shared the same birthday and middle name as my ex-husband. I had six biological children; he now effectively had six as well. The parallels were uncanny, almost divinely orchestrated.

We dated for nearly two years. Some might say that was a long courtship, especially given the intensity of our initial connection. But there were sensitivities, perceptions to consider. People whispered, wondering if we had known each other before his wife's passing. The truth was, our meeting was entirely born out of that Sunday morning at the church, a chain of events set in motion by a dying woman's fervent request. Many who witnessed our story unfold believe that his late wife, in her final act of love, somehow passed her husband on to me, knowing he would be in good hands.

On May 2, 2020, Hugh and I were married. It wasn't a whirlwind, impulsive decision like my first marriage. This was a considered choice, a conscious stepping into a new season with a man whose kindness, softness, and unwavering support had already begun to heal parts of me I thought were irreparably broken.

What struck me most profoundly about Hugh, what set him apart from every man I had ever known, was his profound respect, not just for me, but for all women. My past relationships had been a landscape of disrespect, selfishness, and emotional neglect. Hugh was different. He listened, truly listened. He paid attention. He cherished me. I wasn't used to such focused, consistent care. He'd accompany me to the grocery store, holding my purse as if it were a precious jewel. We attended church together, always. If I had a day off from work, he'd take a day off too, just so we could be together. This constant presence, this "on-my-hip" devotion, which might have felt stifling with another man, felt like a shield with Hugh. It rebuilt my shattered trust, piece by precious piece.

Ministry is my heart, my calling. And Hugh embraced it, not as an obligation, but as a shared passion. He is a computer analyst by trade, yet he serves as the co-pastor of Soul Winners. He's the church handyman, the finance person, the head of the food bank, the organizer of our Amazon donations room. He throws himself into every aspect of the ministry with a humility that astounds me. He's not driven by ego or a need for the spotlight. He consistently defers to me as the founding pastor, never seeking to dominate or overshadow. When people approach, he'll often say, "Let me go get the pastor," or "Let me get Dr. Chambers," always honoring my role, my calling. This kind of egoless partnership in ministry is a rare and precious gift.

He embraced my children as his own. The transition was understandably rough for them at first, still healing from the divorce from their father. Erin, in particular, struggled. But Hugh's patient love, his consistent presence, slowly won them over. Today, he and Erin are the best of friends. He's "Papa" to my grandbabies, and the sight of him, a giant of a man, on the edge of the bed with toddlers snuggled between us, or patiently picking them up for church when Erin can't make it, fills my heart with a quiet joy. He packs barrels of goods to send to my daughter in Jamaica with the same care and attention he gives to packing barrels for his own daughter there, ensuring both are equally provided for. Whatever my children need—a car repair for Najee, gas money or lunch money for Erin during her nursing school days—Hugh is there, without complaint, without hesitation. He is a tower of strength, not just for me, but for our entire blended family.

This marriage, this love, has been a profound agent of healing in my life. It has recalibrated my understanding of what a healthy, godly partnership looks like. I used to look at male pastors with a degree of suspicion, colored by my own painful experiences as a pastor's wife. I pitied their wives, imagining them silenced, suffering in quiet desperation. Hugh has shown me a different way. He has shown me that a man of God can be humble, supportive, respectful, and truly collaborative. He has helped me to release the bitterness, to see men in ministry not as a monolith, but as individuals.

If you had asked me, in the depths of my despair after my divorce, if I believed such a love was possible, I would have likely said no. I had given up on the idea of a healthy, whole love. But God, in His infinite wisdom and boundless grace, had other plans. He sent Hugh, my gentle warrior, my *total package*, not when I was looking, not when I was striving, but when I had finally, completely, surrendered.

To any woman reading this, any woman who has been battered by trauma, hurt, pain, abuse, and betrayal, who has given up on the dream of a love that heals and restores, I would say this: It is not by might, nor by power, but by My Spirit, says the Lord. Don't be too hard on yourself. Don't go desperately searching. Walk in your God-given purpose, whatever that may be. Do it from a pure heart, unto the Lord, not for the eyes of men.

Your gift, the unique essence of who you are, will make room for you. And when you least expect it, when you have finally laid down your own striving, God will supply all your needs, often in ways more beautiful and complete than you could ever have imagined.

What is for you, no one can take from you. Trust His timing. He is the ultimate orchestrator, the Master Weaver, and He can take the most tangled threads of a life and create a tapestry of breathtaking beauty. Hugh is my living proof. He is the love that heals, the partner who champions my calling, the man who embodies the total package—a gift, unexpected and profoundly cherished, from the very heart of God.

SELF-REFLECTION QUESTIONS:

What does a healthy, honoring love look like for you—and where have you accepted less?

Which wounds still shape how you trust, and what would help you let someone love you there?

How will you recognize a partner who protects your purpose rather than competes with it?

What boundaries would make love feel safer, softer, and more sustainable in your life?

If you believed good love could find you without striving, what would you stop doing—and what would you start?

Chapter 18

Illness to Healing

L ife has a way of throwing curveballs when you least expect them, even when you feel like you've finally found your footing, your purpose. Just as I was navigating the complexities of ministry, the joys and challenges of a new marriage, and the ongoing rhythm of family life, my own body began to send out subtle, then increasingly insistent, distress signals. It started insidiously, a slow creep of unease that I initially dismissed, attributing it to stress, to the constant demands on my time and energy.

The early signs were a strange mix of physical and emotional turmoil. I'd find myself inexplicably moody, like a sudden storm cloud passing over a sunny day. One minute I'd be fine, engaged, and energetic; the next, a heavy, suffocating blanket of sadness would descend, leaving me withdrawn and irritable. In Jamaica, we have a word for it—"cross." It's that feeling of being on edge, easily agitated, like every nerve is exposed. That was me. I was just... cross.

Then came the physical manifestations. My heart would often race, a wild, tachycardic rhythm thumping in my chest, sometimes so forceful I could feel it, a frantic bird trapped against my ribs. Hot flashes would wash over me, intense waves of heat that left me feeling flushed and uncomfortable, even in cool rooms. I'd passed menopause years before, so this sudden resurgence of what felt like menopausal symptoms was deeply unsettling. *Is menopause coming back?* I'd wonder, a knot of confusion tightening in my stomach.

Mentally, I was a wreck. A profound sadness, a deep, unshakeable melancholy, became my constant companion. I felt withdrawn, disconnected. The anxiety was the worst, a relentless, suffocating presence. It became so severe that I struggled to make eye contact. Even talking to people, something I did constantly in my ministry, became an ordeal. My hands would shake, my voice would tremble, a nervous energy thrumming just beneath my skin. It got to the point where even a phone conversation could trigger a wave of anxiety, my heart pounding as if I were facing some unseen threat, even though the person on the other end couldn't see me.

The most alarming symptom, the one that truly terrified both me and my husband, Hugh, was the weight loss and the extreme hair loss. It was rapid, relentless. The pounds seemed to melt off me, leaving me gaunt and frail. My eyes, once bright and expressive, began to look sunken, lost in dark hollows. Then came the hair. Not just a little shedding, but handfuls. The shower drain filled. My brush looked like it belonged to someone else. Between the Graves' flare-ups and my alopecia, I watched my edges thin and my part widen.

Hugh, having already lost his late wife to cancer, started to get visibly scared. I could see the fear in his eyes, the unspoken worry that history was repeating itself, that he was about to lose another wife. "Don't tell me," his expression seemed to say, "not again." It was a heavy burden for both of us to bear. Adding to the misery was the frequent urination. It was constant, especially at night. I'd go to the bathroom, only to feel the urge return the moment I started to walk back to bed. It was as if my body was betraying me, every system haywire. And everything I ate seemed to go right through me, which explained the dramatic weight loss.

The emergency room became a grimly familiar destination. Each time my heart rate spiked, my blood pressure would shoot up in response, a terrifying physiological cascade. I'd feel that tell-tale thumping in my chest, the fear would grip me, and my blood pressure would skyrocket. More than once, I had to call 911, my voice trembling as I tried to explain what was happening. Ambulances picked me up from work, from home, rushing me to the hospital. On one occasion, the symptoms were so severe—the racing heart, the disorientation—that they thought I was having a stroke.

But after a battery of tests, CT scans, and EKGs, the doctors would inevitably scratch their heads, find nothing definitively wrong, and send me home with vague reassurances and, sometimes, thinly veiled suspicions. They started asking questions. "Is someone hurting you at home, Pastor Chambers?" The implication was clear: they thought my symptoms might be psychosomatic, a manifestation of domestic stress, or worse, that I was simply crazy.

And the heartbreaking part was, I started to believe them. My ex-husband, during the tumultuous end of our marriage, had certainly insinuated that I was losing my mind. Even some people at church, witnessing my unexplained physical decline and my emotional fragility, began to whisper. And in the lonely, frightening echo chamber of my own thoughts, a terrible doubt began to take root. *The doctors can't find anything wrong. My heart is jumping out of my chest. I'm having hot flashes when I shouldn't be. Am I... am I going crazy?*

It was a lot for us to handle, for me and for Hugh. I remember one particular Saturday morning. I was at home, trying to go about my usual chores, cleaning the house. Suddenly, my heart started that wild, frantic dance in my chest. The hot flashes came, one after another, consuming me, making me feel like I was burning up from the inside out. "No," I gasped, leaning against the counter for support, "I can't do this anymore." I drove myself to the emergency room, desperate for answers, for relief, for someone to finally tell me what was wrong with me. And that day, finally, they did.

After yet another round of blood work, a doctor came in with a diagnosis: hyperthyroidism. Not hypothyroidism, the more common and generally manageable form where the thyroid is underactive. No, I had hyperthyroidism, where the thyroid gland is overactive, kicking every system in the body into overdrive. It explained everything: the racing heart, the anxiety, the weight loss, the frequent urination, the hair loss, the mental fog. It was, the doctor explained, a serious condition, one that could affect every organ in my body, especially my mental state. Anxiety, she confirmed, was a primary side effect. She prescribed medication immediately and referred me for further testing. Within two months, the diagnosis was refined: Graves' disease.

"Graves' disease," I repeated. I knew the name. I remembered Wendy Williams, the talk show host, and her public struggles with the same condition. I knew it could cause the eyes to bulge, a symptom I was thankfully spared, though my eyes were often affected in other ways. I knew it was an autoimmune disorder, a relentless internal battle. With Graves' disease, stress is your enemy. Any kind of stress, emotional or physical, can trigger a flare-up, sending your system into that terrifying overdrive. Even now, if I get too agitated, too stressed, I can feel that familiar nervousness creeping in, my words getting tangled, my thoughts racing. It's a constant reminder that my body is working overtime.

But in that moment, hearing the diagnosis—hyperthyroidism, Graves' disease—I didn't feel despair. Strangely, I felt an overwhelming sense of relief. Finally. Finally, I had a name for the invisible monster that had been tormenting me. Finally, I knew I wasn't crazy. Finally, there was a path forward, a way to fight back. For so long, I had been adrift in a sea of unexplained symptoms, doubted by doctors, whispered about by my own church family. Now, at least, I knew what I was dealing with and what to tell them.

The doctors laid out the options: surgery to remove my thyroid or medication to manage the condition. I opted for the medication, hoping it would bring my runaway system back into balance. And I put my trust in God. "Lord," I prayed, "let Your will be done in this situation." I wasn't demanding healing, not in an anxious or fearful way. I was surrendering, trusting that He would guide and sustain me.

But if I'm being honest, there was a part of me that felt a deep, simmering disappointment, not at God, but at some of my loved ones, the ones I poured my heart into serving. I am the founder of Soul Winners Pentecostal Church, the visionary. For twenty years, I had given everything to this ministry. I was always the first one at the hospital when a member was sick, the first one at the jailhouse when someone got into trouble, the first one to offer a helping hand, whatever it took. I was on the front lines, always, despite my health challenges. And yet, in my own moment of profound vulnerability, when I was down, when I desperately needed someone to pick me up, to offer comfort, to simply believe me, that's when some criticism, ostracism, the whispers, had been the loudest. I remember feeling so ashamed, my weight plummeting, my clothes hanging off my skeletal frame, feeling like I was "twirling around in my dresses," as we say. The pastor, the leader, and no one knew what was wrong with her. It was humiliating.

And the prophets, the prayer warriors, the ones who claimed such deep spiritual insight—none of them, not one, had been able to discern the true nature of my illness, to offer a prayer of healing that brought relief, or even to simply point me in the right direction medically. It felt like a profound failure, not on my part, but on the part of the spiritual community. It was then, in my deepest hurt, that I truly understood the scripture: "Let the church be the church." But sometimes, I realized with a heavy heart, the church forgets its true calling.

I believe, with all my heart, that it's often the quiet ones, the unassuming, faithful remnants in the corner, the ones nobody pays much attention to, who are the truest reflection of Christ. All the noise, the eloquent preaching, the displays of spiritual authority, the beautiful singing—if it's not rooted in genuine, compassionate love, it means nothing. It's a facade. It's self-serving. When one of your own is down, you don't pull away; you rally to lift them up. I share this not to cast blame, but to highlight a painful truth and to encourage the church at large that charity begins at home.

The medication began to take effect. Slowly, gradually, my body started to respond. After about nine months to a year, I went into remission. Unlike Wendy Williams, unlike the Jamaican singer Vybz Kartel, who also battles Graves', I was blessed. My healing, I believe, came not just from the medication, but from a deep well of honesty with God, from a stubborn faithfulness, from a genuine love for Him that persisted even in the darkest days. So many people offer lip service to faith, quick to "plead the blood" without the corresponding heart of humility and surrender. God expects His true children to be humble, to trust His will, not to try and "boss Him around" with demanding prayers. I didn't resist, I didn't rebel, I didn't fight God. I humbly went to Him and said, "Lord, let Your will be done."

Even in remission, which I claim as my healing by the Lord, the doctors warned me that I could still experience "thyroid eye," a common complication of Graves'. It's a condition another Jamaican runner, whose name escapes me now, also advocates for. This is why this book, this story, feels so important. So many people talk about cancer, about diabetes, about mental health struggles. But Graves' disease, hyperthyroidism—these often remain in the shadows, misunderstood, misdiagnosed. People generalize "thyroid problems," not understanding the critical difference between "hypo" (underactive, often leading to weight gain and sluggishness) and "hyper" (overactive, a raging internal storm). Life insurance companies know the difference; premiums for those with hyperthyroidism are significantly higher.

One of the lingering effects for me, even in remission, has been with my eyes and a persistent tiredness. For a long time, I'd see a little black pencil-like floater moving in the corner of my left eye. And the fatigue... oh, the fatigue is profound. Graves' disease means everything in your body is working overtime, and that takes a tremendous toll. I always have this tired look, a weariness etched into my face. There were times, many times, when I'd go out, and people would stare. Some even asked, point-blank, if I was on drugs, if I was smoking weed. Their judgment, their unspoken accusations, would crush me, send me spiraling back into that pit of shame and anxiety. If I don't get enough rest, even now, that tired look returns, a visible reminder of the invisible battle my body has fought and, in some ways, continues to fight.

It used to devastate me, this feeling of being constantly scrutinized, misunderstood. I was used to being bubbly, vibrant, a go-getter. Now, I often felt like retreating into a shell, wondering what people were seeing, what they were thinking. But I learned something crucial through all of this: you cannot judge a book by its cover. Not everyone who looks tired is lazy. Not everyone who seems withdrawn is unfriendly. Not everyone who appears "off" is on drugs. We, especially those of us in the church, need to cultivate a spirit of discernment, of compassion, of withholding judgment. If you know someone, if you've seen them vibrant and full of life, and then you see a drastic change, don't assume the worst. Ask. Reach out. Offer support. If someone had told me they were diagnosed with a rare disease I knew nothing about, I would have immediately gone home and researched it, trying to understand, trying to see how I could help. That's what love does. And sadly, sometimes, people just don't love hard enough. It often feels like the "strong friend," the one who is always giving, always serving, is the one who gets the short end of the stick when they themselves are in need.

But through this fiery trial, I learned to manage. I learned to advocate for myself. I learned the critical importance of self-care. Even when I felt my worst, I made a conscious effort to take care of myself. Going to the hairdresser, feeling the soothing warmth of the water on my scalp, the gentle massage—those simple acts became sacred rituals, moments of respite that made me feel human again, cherished. Massages were a godsend, easing the tension, calming the anxiety. I also became a gym freak. When I couldn't make it to the gym, my bathroom became my sanctuary, where I'd blast music and do Zumba or step aerobics. Exercise was, and is, a powerful antidote to the mental and physical toll of this disease.

And I served. I poured myself into the ministry, into the food bank, into organizing donations in our Amazon room. Seeing the gratitude on the faces of those we helped, knowing I was making a tangible difference, took my mind off my own struggles. I also completely overhauled my diet. I cut out starches, sugars, rice, red meat, and pork. I focused on fish, brown rice, and an abundance of fruits and vegetables, especially smoothies packed with blueberries, strawberries, oranges, and cucumbers. I believe, with all my heart, that these lifestyle changes played a significant role in my journey to remission.

This season of illness didn't diminish my faith; if anything, it deepened it, refined it. It taught me about boundaries, about the necessity of self-care, about the importance of slowing down, even when the world, and sometimes my own inner drive, urged me to keep pushing. My identity shifted. I was no longer just Pastor Chambers, the strong leader. I was also Anglore, a woman battling a chronic illness, a woman learning to be vulnerable, to receive care as well as give it.

To any woman out there who is balancing illness and purpose, who is juggling the demands of ministry or family or career with the relentless challenges of a chronic condition, I say this: You are one of a kind. Your fingerprint, your blueprint, is unique. Find your strength within yourself, within your connection to God. Don't wait for external validation. Endorse yourself. Know your worth. Be transparent. Be real. Be authentic. Tell your truth, even when it's hard, even when it's painful. Don't be afraid. What happens in darkness will eventually come to light. The only person who can truly destroy you is YOU. Walk in your purpose, whatever that may be. You are strong. So stand strong. Be solid as a rock. Don't be a fraud, don't be fake. Do what you do because you want to do it, because God has called you to it, not because someone else is influencing you. Be a leader, not a follower. Be you. And if you need help, ask for it. Never be ashamed. A closed mouth doesn't get fed. It's better to ask than to suffer in silence or resort to desperate measures. Take what you need, go on your merry way, and don't you dare worry about what anyone else is going to say about you.

The practical tools that helped me survive and heal were many: my faith, first and foremost. The scriptures became my daily bread. I love to study, to research, to delve into theology. Everything we face in life, good or bad, is addressed in the Bible. It's a wellspring of comfort, wisdom, and peace. But for those who may not yet know God in that way, I'd say: find a true friend. And find comfort and healing in the act of helping others. Even if you have nothing, give out of your nothing. Cook a meal for a shelter. Visit someone in the hospital. I don't care how dire your own situation is; there is always someone in a worse predicament. Reaching out, being a blessing, even in your own pain, has a profoundly healing effect. It shifts your focus from your own suffering to the needs of others, and in that selfless act, you often find your own strength, your own peace.

My pain, this journey through Graves' disease, has undeniably become a deeper layer of my purpose. Just recently, I was speaking to a young lady going through a terribly rough time, and I saw so much of my own past struggles in her eyes. I told her about this book, about the journey I've been on, and I could see a flicker of hope ignite in her. To be able to testify, especially to women, but also to men and even to my own children, that what I went through has become a source of strength and blessing—that is the ultimate redemption. God set me up, took me through the fire, so that I could sit with others in their pain and say, "Listen, the God who brought me through is able to bring you through too. If He did it for me, He can do it for you. Have hope. Be hopeful. God is able." That, in essence, is the heart of my healing, and the continuing call of my ministry.

SELF-REFLECTION QUESTIONS:

What is your body trying to tell you right now that you've been minimizing or pushing past?

How do you want others to support you during flare-ups or hard days—and have you told them clearly?

Where do you need to set (or strengthen) a boundary so healing has space without guilt?

Which practice—prayer, journaling, breathwork, quiet walks—actually calms your fear when symptoms spike?

If your titles and productivity were stripped away for a season, who are you—and what truth will you stand on?

Conclusion

The Smile Behind the Pain

Looking back on the winding, often treacherous path of my life, if you were to ask me what memory first surfaces when I think of the very beginning of this journey, it's not a single image but a full-bodied experience of pain, shame, and sheer survival. The memory that has, in many ways, become the foundational stone of my entire story is the birth of my second daughter, the one who still resides in Jamaica. She was born not in a sterile hospital room or even a humble, prepared home, but in the cold, damp confines of an outdoor pit latrine.

I can still feel the hard-packed earth beneath my knees, the sharp, relentless cramps that seized my young body—a body that was still a mystery to me in so many ways. I was barely a woman myself, just eighteen or nineteen, yet I was bringing another life into this world, a world that had shown me precious little kindness. I was homeless, having fled one untenable situation for another, and I was hungry with a desperation that only a pregnant woman can truly know. And I was utterly alone in my secret. To survive, I had learned to hide, to bind my growing belly so tightly with cloth that my pregnancy remained invisible to the world, even to the uncle who had given me temporary shelter. But a baby's arrival cannot be hidden forever. I remember the shock of seeing blood, the raw, animalistic fear that gripped me as I realized what was happening. My cries for help, torn from a place of sheer terror, brought my uncle running. I can still see the look on his face—a mixture of confusion, shock, and helplessness. He didn't know. No one knew. It was a kind neighbor, a woman summoned in a panic, who finally gave voice to the truth: "She's having a baby."

In that moment, I felt a shame so profound it threatened to swallow me whole. There was no preparation. No neatly folded baby clothes, no diapers, no receiving blankets waiting to swaddle new life. There was nothing but the stark, raw reality of birth, attended by a local midwife who was summoned in a rush. I felt less than human, as if I were no different from an animal in the wild, giving birth unprepared and alone. That experience, that deep, searing pain, became the genesis of my smile. The smile became my shield, my camouflage. Even as I was pregnant and starving, wandering from place to place, I learned to smile. I had to. It was a survival mechanism, a mask to hide the tears that were always just beneath the surface. Over the decades, I mastered that smile. It became my default setting, a way to navigate a world that often felt hostile and unforgiving. I smiled through homelessness in New York, my feet aching from walking the streets all day just to afford a few hours in a dingy hotel room at night. I smiled through abusive relationships, my heart breaking behind a carefully constructed facade of contentment. I smiled through the quiet judgment and whispers in the church, my spirit crying out for understanding even as my lips curved upwards.

That hidden pain, those private battles fought in the shadows, became the very thing that shaped the strength and fierce determination I possess today. The memory of being pregnant and hungry is a fire that has never gone out. I remember standing under a mango tree in Spanish Town, my stomach a hollow, aching void, praying with every fiber of my being for just one piece of fruit to fall. That is not a memory you forget. It is why I cannot, will not, ever turn my nose up at anyone in need. It's why our church's food bank is not just a program to me; it is a sacred mission, a direct response to the deepest pain of my past.

If I could reach back through time and speak to that scared, eighteen-year-old girl—the one giving birth in a pit toilet, the one hiding her shame from the world—I wouldn't scold her for her choices or her fear. I would wrap my arms around her and whisper, "You did a good job. You did what you had to do to survive, and because of your fight, your daughter is alive today. What you are going through right now, this pain that feels so unbearable it might break you, is a stepping stone. It feels like a curse, but it is a pruning. God is using this very moment to shape you, to cut away everything that is not of Him, so that He can mold you into the powerful woman He created you to be." For so long, I was deeply ashamed of that part of my story. Now, I see it as one of my greatest breakthroughs. If I could survive that, if God could bring me through that crucible, there is nothing on this earth that can truly break me. That pain, once a source of unbearable shame, has bred a power inside of me that I didn't even know I possessed.

And there are other pains, other secrets I carried in silence for years, that also contributed to the weight behind my smile. I must be honest with you, my reader, because my healing is incomplete if I am not wholly truthful. In the tumultuous years of my youth, lost in a cycle of hurt and survival, I made the painful decision to have an abortion. For decades, the guilt and shame of my choices were a heavy shroud over my spirit. I felt a chasm between myself and God, convinced that He was angry with me, that I was irrevocably stained, unworthy of His love, and certainly unworthy of His calling. I know, with every fiber of my being, that I am not alone in this. So many people, especially within the body of Christ, allow the shame of past abortion, past hurts, and past mistakes to cripple them. They live in a self-imposed prison of guilt, believing the lie that their past disqualifies them from their future, that they are unworthy to complete their earthly assignments or to walk in obedience to their calling.

I am here to tell you that is a lie from the pit of hell. The journey to healing from that specific pain was long and arduous, and it began with one crucial step: I had to learn to forgive myself. I had to release the condemnation that I had held onto so tightly, the belief that God could never use a woman like me for ministry. But He has. He has taken my brokenness and used it for His glory. If you are carrying a similar burden, please hear me: God's grace is bigger than your biggest mistake. His forgiveness is more powerful than your deepest shame. He is not holding it against you; the only one holding it against you is you.

Through this long and arduous journey, through all the suffering and the unexpected triumphs, I have learned profound truths, lessons not taught in any classroom or sermon, but forged in the fires of real life. These are the truths I now live by.

First, I have learned that **I can do all things through Christ who strengthens me.** This is not a mere platitude or a hopeful affirmation; it is the very bedrock of my existence. It's the truth that gets me out of bed on days when weariness threatens to keep me down. It's the promise I clung to when the boiler in our church broke in the dead of winter, when the pipes burst and we were displaced. In that moment of crisis, when everything seemed lost, it was this truth that fueled my determination. I remember thinking, *A father who does not take care of his family is worse than an infidel. And God,*

You are my Father. You said it Yourself. You are the ultimate example. I stood on His word, and He made a way where there was no way.

Second, I have learned that **with Christ in the vessel, I can smile at the storm.** This has been the central theme of my life. For years, my smile was a mask, a way to hide the tempest raging within. But through a genuine, transformative relationship with Jesus, the nature of my smile changed. It is no longer a cover for pain, but a reflection of the unshakeable peace that resides within me. The storms still come—they always will—but now, I am not in the boat alone. Christ is in the vessel of my life, and His presence gives me the supernatural ability to face the wind and the waves not with fear, but with a deep, abiding peace that passes all understanding. My smile, now, is genuine. It is the smile of a survivor, a victor, a woman who knows that the one who is in her is greater than any storm in the world.

And third, I have learned that **it ain't over until God says it's over.** How many times have I been brought to what I thought was the absolute, undeniable end? When my first marriage dissolved after thirty years, when the church I had poured my life into experienced a split that saw nearly ninety percent of the congregation walk away, when my body was ravaged by an illness that doctors couldn't diagnose—in each of those moments, a part of me thought, *This is it. I'm done.* But time and time again, just when I thought the story had reached its final, tragic chapter, God would turn the page. He would open a new door, provide a new resource, send a new person. He has taught me that human endings are not God's endings. His plans for us are always greater than our current circumstances, and as long as there is breath in our lungs, His purpose for our lives is still unfolding.

The greatest lesson of all has been one of perseverance, of unwavering faith, and of a stubborn, unyielding will to overcome. My success today is not defined by any worldly standard, not by the size of our church building or by any accolades I might receive. Success, for me, is rooted in a high self-esteem that comes not from pride, but from a deep, unshakable knowledge of who I am in Christ. It's the ability to fail, to fall flat on your face, and to get back up, dust yourself off, and say, "Let's try again." It's the profound understanding that you were fearfully and wonderfully made by the Great I Am. I am a fighter because life has demanded it of me. I am not a loser; I must win, not for my own glory, but for His. And now, when people try to weigh me down with the baggage of my past, when they whisper and judge, I can smile a true smile and think to myself, "If I put that baggage down, it's because it was too heavy for me to carry. If you want to pick it up and try to carry it, go right ahead. But be warned, it will likely kill you."

To anyone reading this who is facing their own struggles, to anyone who is hiding their own deep and private pain behind a weary, practiced smile, I want to offer this encouragement: find your own strength, the strength that God has already placed within you, and just keep pushing forward. Your current circumstances do not define your final destination. Your pain has a profound purpose. It is not happening *to* you; it is happening *for* you. It is the very thing that is shaping you, preparing you, building in you a resilience and a depth of character you never knew you had. Remember the promise: what the devil means for evil, God will always, always turn around for your good.

My pain mattered because it was necessary. It was the fire that forged me, the relentless pressure that turned a worthless lump of coal into something of value. It was the necessary prerequisite for my promotion in the Kingdom, the grueling, hands-on training ground for my ultimate purpose. You simply cannot have a powerful testimony without first enduring a test.

In closing, I offer this blessing to every single reader who has made it to this final page, to every soul who has journeyed with me through the valleys and the mountaintops of my story: I decree and I declare, in the powerful and matchless name of Jesus, that God will deposit multiplied blessings, favor, and grace into your hearts. I decree and declare the divine protection and unwavering provision of Psalm 91 and the steadfast guidance and help of Psalm 121 over your lives, not just for a season, but for all the days of your lives, until we meet in glory. Amen.

SELF-REFLECTION QUESTIONS:

Which parts of your story still ache—and what truth do you need to speak over them today?

When has pain secretly grown your strength, faith, or compassion? Name one lesson you're taking forward.

What support (person, practice, or place) will you lean on when the next hard season comes?

Where are you still "smiling to cope" instead of "smiling with honesty"? What would courageous honesty look like this week?

What is one small, doable step you will take in the next 24 hours to honor your healing and keep moving?

Epilogue

A s I sit here now, in the quiet of my home, a gentle peace settles over me like a
warm blanket. The frantic energy of survival, the constant, gnawing anxiety that
was my companion for so many years, has been replaced by a deep, abiding calm. I look
at my husband, Hugh, my gentle warrior, and I see the physical embodiment of God's
restorative love. I hear the sound of my grandchildren's laughter echoing through the
house, a sound so pure and joyous it feels like a melody from heaven itself. This is my
now. A life of peace, of love, of purpose. When I contrast this beautiful, stable present
with the chaotic, painful past I've just recounted, the journey seems almost impossible, a
story too incredible to be true. But it is true. And it is a testament not to my own strength,
but to the relentless, redeeming grace of an awesome God. To you, my dear reader, who
has so generously given your time and your heart to journey with me through these pages,
I want to leave you with a few final thoughts, a word from my spirit to yours, something
to carry with you as you close this book and continue on your own unique and sacred
path.

Please know, with every fiber of your being, that life is not a bed of roses, and challenges
are inevitable. There is no such thing as a problem-free life, no magical destination where
all our troubles cease. Even Jesus Christ, the Son of God, experienced profound agony. On
the cross, He cried out, "My God, my God, why hast thou forsaken me?" In the Garden of
Gethsemane, He asked His closest friends, "Could you not stay up with me and pray for
just one hour?" He, too, faced storms. He never promised us a life without tempests, but
He did promise to be with us in the boat, to never leave us nor forsake us. These challenges
are not meant to destroy you; they are life lessons, an essential, and often painful, part of

your development. They are the very tools God uses to shape you, to mold you, to build a character and a resilience within you that you could never achieve in a life of ease.

I have learned that there is an immense power in your smile. For years, my smile was a mask, a way to cover a multitude of pains. But as I healed, as I grew in my faith and in my understanding of my own worth, the nature of my smile transformed. It is no longer just a shield; it is now a weapon of joy, a conscious choice to radiate hope, a tangible representation of the victory I have won in Christ. But I also implore you, be intentional. When you see someone else's smile, don't take it at face value. Look deeper. See the story behind their eyes. Ask how they're really doing. A smile can be a language of its own, sometimes a cry for help disguised as happiness.

Remember that everything you are searching for—love, validation, purpose, strength—is already within you. For too long, I looked for my worth in the eyes of others, in the acceptance of men, in the approval of the church. But true fulfillment only came when I learned to look in the mirror and see the woman God created me to be. You must learn to encourage yourself, to validate yourself, to know your worth in Christ, independent of anyone else's opinion. You are fearfully and wonderfully made. You are enough. And please, never, ever believe the insidious lie that it's too late. You are never too old. You may be delayed, but you are never denied. I found the truest, most healing love of my life when many would have considered me past my prime. I am publishing my first book as I approach my seventieth birthday. God's timing is not our timing, but I promise you, it is always perfect. He is never in a rush, but He is always on time. And what you look like on the outside—whether you are young or old, tired from illness or vibrant with health, whether you fit the world's standards of beauty or not—does not, and cannot, define the immense power, the unique purpose, and the breathtaking beauty that God has placed within you.

So, what's next for me? The journey, I am thrilled to say, is far from over. The vision that now consumes my waking thoughts and my most fervent prayers is to build shelters for homeless women and their children. My heart aches for the women who are where I once was—scared, alone, and with nowhere to turn. The church building has the physical space; God has given me the vision. I am now stepping out in faith, trusting Him to provide the resources, the connections, and the favor to turn this dream into a tangible reality, a true haven for those in desperate need. And, of course, there is The Red Shoe Experience Conference! This is a vision that has been growing in my heart for some time, a powerful, one-day conference dedicated to the empowerment and rejuvenation of women. It will be a day of pampering, yes, with massages, workshops, and opportunities to rest and recharge. But more importantly, it will be a day to learn about the incredible power of resilience, to discover how to walk through your pain and emerge on the other side stronger, more beautiful, and more aligned with your God-given purpose. The red shoes, once a symbol of a painful, transactional moment in my youth, will be reclaimed as a symbol of victory, of empowerment, of stepping boldly into the future God has for us. You may come in feeling empty, but I guarantee, you will leave full.

My life has been a testament to the fact that our greatest pain points can become our greatest platforms for purpose. My prayer for you, as I close this chapter of my story, is that you will look at your own life, at your own scars, and see them not as marks of shame, but as proof of your survival, as the very credentials that qualify you to minister to a hurting world. Thank you, from the bottom of my heart, for walking this road with me. My deepest prayer is that my story has inspired you, encouraged you, and served as a powerful reminder that no matter how deep the pain, no matter how dark the night, healing is not just possible; it is your birthright. Purpose can and will be found in the most unlikely of places. And victory, in the end, is always, always yours for the taking. Now, go and let your own unique, beautiful, and resilient light shine brighter than ever before.

Final Words

As you close this book, I want to leave you with a final word, a message that flows from the deepest parts of my experiences. I am a firm believer in the transformative power of forgiveness. I know that there may be some who have waited for this book to come out, perhaps hoping, or even expecting, that I would use these pages as a tool to settle old scores, to hurt those who have hurt me. But I must be clear: this book is not an instrument of revenge. It is not in my heart, not in my spiritual DNA, to seek vengeance or to delight in the pain of others.

I was talking to my husband the other day, and I told him, if, God forbid, someone were to physically harm or even kill one of my children—a thought that is every mother's worst nightmare—my response would be different from what the world expects. We see it on the news: grieving family members understandably demanding that the perpetrator be put away for life, to rot in jail. And while I understand that raw, human desire for justice, my heart, shaped by a lifetime of both receiving and needing grace, would lead me down a different path. I would appeal to the court system not to simply lock that person away and throw away the key. My belief is that for an individual to commit such a heinous act, there must be a profound sickness within them, a deep brokenness, a cry for help that has gone unheard. I would ask the court to find the best possible help for that person, to put them in a hospital or a mental health facility, to seek restoration rather than mere retribution.

My job on this earth, as I see it, is to restore. Vengeance belongs to God; He will repay. This is not my burden to carry. When someone hurts you, God Himself is more than capable of handling the situation in His own time and in His own way. Nothing takes

Him by surprise. The things that happen to us in this life, as painful as they may be, are often a part of our destiny, orchestrated by God to strengthen us, to shape us, to prepare us for our purpose. And so, forgiveness is my motto.

I can sit here today and tell you of the ugly, painful, and unjust things that have been done to me, and I know I could have sought revenge. I could have used my words, my influence, my story to hurt them in return. But it has never been in my spirit to do that. The Bible tells me that God looks beyond our faults every day and sees our needs, and He still supplies them, in spite of our own evil, our own shortcomings. If God's motive is always to restore, then my motive must be to restore as well.

This book is meant to encourage, to inspire, to teach. It is a testament to the fact that you do not have to waste your precious time and energy trying to hurt an individual who has wronged you. You never truly know the reason behind their actions. You don't know what is going on with them mentally, what hidden battles they are fighting. Perhaps their hurtful actions are a desperate, misguided cry for help. And if, in our own pain, we respond with revenge, we may be adding more hurt to an already wounded soul, and in doing so, we might just push them over the edge.

I want this book to speak to the world at large, and especially to the church. God so loved the world that He did not come to condemn it, but that through Him, the world might be saved. His motive is love. And if love is His motive, it must be ours as well. We must allow love to preside over evil in our own hearts. We cannot walk around with unforgiveness festering within us, for these things—bitterness, resentment, the desire for revenge—will eventually kill our spirit and send us to a place we do not want to go. This is my motive. This is what I want this book to do: to speak to the world, to speak to the church, and to say, do not be so quick to expose, to judge, to seek revenge, to hurt people. Don't do it.

And this process of forgiveness, so essential to our healing, must begin with one crucial first step: we must forgive ourselves. I am hoping and praying that as a people, and especially as the church, we can learn how to forgive ourselves first. Once you have extended that grace to your own soul, you will then be able to freely and genuinely forgive others. That is my prayer for you.

My final, final word is to the church. There is a saying, and I believe it is biblical in its spirit: "United we stand, divided we fall." When we, the Body of Christ, are divided, we open the door for the enemy to come in and kill, steal, and destroy—to kill our families, to kill our communities, to kill our God-given purposes. And so, I am making a heartfelt appeal to the church at large. I do not care what your denomination is. Whether you are United Pentecostal, Baptist, Methodist, Catholic, Muslim, Jehovah's Witness—I don't care what sign is over your door. I am making an appeal for us to come together as one. For when we come together as one body, united in the love of Christ, we are a force to be reckoned with. That is my final word.

Maya Angelou's Poem

*J*ust *Give Me a Cool Drink of Water 'fore I Diiie* is a collection filled with themes of love, longing, resilience, racial struggle, and the essence of the human experience. The title itself conveys a sense of urgency, yearning, and survival, reflecting the thirst for relief, justice, or connection in the face of hardship. Her work often captures the ache of unfulfilled needs, the sting of injustice, and the enduring spirit required to navigate adversity. Like Maya, my work, my life, and everything I did was about survival—not just bare, awful, plodding survival, but survival with grace and faith. While one may encounter many defeats, one must not be defeated.

As I reflect on her words, I see the parallels in my own journey. Like Angelou, I've experienced moments of longing, not just for love, but for purpose and fulfillment. I, too, have navigated struggles that tested my resilience, and I have drawn strength from the lessons they taught me. Angelou's work reminds me that the thirst for more—for connection, for understanding, for wholeness—is not a weakness. Her ability to turn pain into poetry inspires me to transform my own experiences into stories that resonate with others.

In her acclaimed autobiography, *I Know Why the Caged Bird Sings*, Maya Angelou shared that at the age of 8, she was sexually abused and raped by her mother's boyfriend, a man named Freeman. Maya stated, "I told my brother, who told the rest of the family." Freeman was found guilty but was jailed for only one day. Four days after his release, he was murdered, probably by Angelou's uncles. Angelou became mute for almost five years, believing, as she stated, "I thought my voice killed him; I killed that man because I told his name, and then I thought I would never speak again, because my voice would kill anyone."

According to biographer Marcia Ann-Gillespie and her colleagues, it was during this period of silence that Angelou developed her extraordinary memory, her love for books and literature, and her ability to listen and observe the world around her. As a result, she became positive. My accuser, who sexually assaulted me at 8 years old, is still walking around and was never confronted for that evil act. Today, I still carry the shame of his wicked selfishness... Such an act of evil should not be tolerated. I pray that mothers will pay close attention to their daughters and granddaughters and pour into them.

In my own creative journey, whether through writing or empowering others, I find myself channeling the same sense of urgency and purpose that Angelou so powerfully embodied. Her words remind me that our voices have the power to heal, connect, and uplift. Just as she used her art to capture the essence of resilience and hope, I strive to do the same, finding my voice and sharing it unapologetically with the world.

About the author

ANGLORE CHAMBERS was born in the lush, vibrant parish of St. Ann, Jamaica, West Indies, and migrated to the United States in 1978. Her voice and values have been profoundly shaped by the rich tapestry of her Jamaican upbringing, particularly by the enduring example of her mother.

One of Anglore's most cherished childhood memories is of her mother cooking in a large pot, always preparing more food than the family needed. When asked why, her mother would simply say, *"Just in case someone stops by and they're hungry."* This simple act of foresight and generosity instilled in Anglore a deep-seated love for community and a servant's heart—a principle that continues to guide her life and ministry today.

Anglore's life mission is to serve as a catalyst for transformation, impacting people's lives in a way that encourages them to become better versions of themselves and to operate from a place of genuine love. She believes that what is done from the heart is what truly germinates and multiplies.

It was through her own profound moments of pain—times of sadness, hunger, and homelessness—that she realized her purpose. These experiences, she now understands, were the best and worst times of her life, forging in her an unshakeable empathy and providing her with the tools to advocate fiercely for those less fortunate.

She feels most called to serve women and those experiencing homelessness—a passion born directly from her own harrowing experiences of being pregnant and homeless. The memory of that deep, gnawing hunger, compounded by the vulnerability of pregnancy, has fueled her lifelong commitment to ensuring that other women in similar situations are met with compassion and practical assistance.

Anglore is the visionary founder of **Soul Winners Pentecostal Church**, located at 1913 Freemansburg Avenue in Easton, Pennsylvania. The name *"Soul Winners"* reflects the church's core mission: to cater to the total person—mind, body, and soul. Anglore firmly believes that while the soul is paramount, you cannot effectively minister to a person's spiritual needs while ignoring their physical hunger or mental anguish.

Thus, Soul Winners is a place of warm praise and worship—but it is also a place where a hot meal is served after the service, embodying the principle that ministry must be holistic.

A dedicated professional in the healthcare field for over three decades, Anglore is a nurse whose compassion has been shaped by years on the front lines of human suffering. Her journey through **Graves' disease** has only deepened her empathy and resolve, teaching her invaluable lessons about resilience, self-care, and the power of faith in the face of physical adversity.

Today, Anglore is a proud wife, mother of six, and grandmother. She is supported in her life and ministry by her loving husband and co-pastor, **Hugh Chambers**, who walks alongside her in every endeavor. She has been recognized for her extensive community service, receiving a **proclamation from the Mayor of the City of Allentown** for her tireless work.

The scripture that anchors her is **Psalm 118:8 (KJV):**
"It is better to trust in the Lord than to put confidence in man."

Her speaking tone is a unique blend of strength and tenderness—bold and straight-forward, yet warm, comforting, and deeply loving.

If Anglore could leave readers with one sentence to remember, it would be a simple yet profound truth she has learned to live by:

"No matter what, just forgive, so you can be forgiven."

Through her writing, Anglore Chambers fills a crucial gap for readers—offering not just a story of survival, but a raw, honest, and ultimately triumphant roadmap to finding purpose in pain, strength in surrender, and healing through the unwavering grace of God.

Notes

www.ingramcontent.com/pod-product-compliance
Lightning Source LLC
Chambersburg PA
CBHW071751120626
46550CB00002B/750